ASSYRIA -

THE FORGOTTEN

NATION

IN PROPHECY!

*God's Word guarantees that BEFORE
the endtime hour of spiritual history comes to
pass, Assyrians will once again have their own
country!*

by

JOHN BOOKO

First Printing: August, 1992
Second Printing: September, 1993
Third Printing: March, 1994

Published by
John Booko Ministries
200 S. Hooker Avenue
Three Rivers, Michigan 49093
(616) 279-2672

Printed in the United States of America.

ASSYRIA -

THE FORGOTTEN NATION

IN PROPHECY!

by
JOHN BOOKO

Burnell Booko, in Assyria, Michigan, (located about 100 miles west of Detroit on Highway 66).

DEDICATION

To my Assyrian mother, Phoebe, who dedicated me, her first born, to God, from whom I learned the Assyrian language and from whose lap I learned of the God of my fathers.

By her intercessory prayers, I was led to receive Jesus Christ as my Savior and Lord in the United States Navy.

I dedicate this book to her, and for the glory of God.

ATTENTION

Bible Group Leaders,
Bible Colleges,
and
Churches

It is our belief that this book contains such powerful prophetic, revelation truths that it should be in the hands of as many as possible.

Your local church, Bible college, etc., can order this book in quantity, and receive special volume discounts. Volume breakdowns are as follows:

1-4   copies: $7.95 each + S&H $2.00
5-10 copies: $7.00 each + S&H $3.00
11-19 copies: $6.00 each + S&H $4.00
20 + copies: $5.00 each + S&H $5.00
100 or more: Call for quote.

To order, please contact:

Reverend John Booko
200 S. Hooker Avenue
Three Rivers, Michigan 49093
(616) 279-2672

TABLE OF CONTENTS

INTRODUCTION

THE MIGRATION OF ASSYRIAN CHRISTIANS

There is a <u>HIDDEN SCRIPTURE</u> which seems to have been forgotten by many biblical scholars, yet its meaning and content are not forgotten by God.

Of course, it is not really hidden in the Bible - it is more precisely a FORGOTTEN scripture - a scripture that is like the missing piece of the gigantic puzzle we call "the endtime hour of spiritual history."

Most Christians have a fairly good understanding about the God-given role of Israel in prophecy, but when they first hear that God has a special place in His plan for Assyria, they are astounded!

"Assyria? How can that be?"

Then, when I explain how the Assyrian nation fits into the endtime puzzle, they rejoice to know that Assyria's role in endtime events truly is the missing piece of the Middle East puzzle that no one seemed to be able to complete.

Assyria fulfills God's prophetic plan, and completes a full, prophetic picture about the Middle East (see Isaiah 19:23-25).

But before I discuss this HIDDEN SCRIPTURE with you in this book, and before I share its **significant prophetic implications**, let me provide you with some background information about my nationality, and a little about my own, personal testimony as an Assyrian American.

Like so many others born into other nationalities, I have nothing to brag about; after all, I had nothing to do with my being an Assyrian.

It just happened.

I was born that way.

So, if I sound in any way like I am boasting about my heritage, I assure you that I am not, because the Word tells us in 1 Corinthians 4:7:

> *"For who maketh thee to differ from another? and what hast thou that thou didst not receive? now if thou didst receive it, why doest thou glory, as if thou hadst not received it?"*

So, I am not boasting about anything except in God.

Having stated that I am an Assyrian, you should know that I am an Assyrian born in the right place. I must admit that sometimes I pray and ask God, "Lord, how come I was so blessed to be born in Chicago, Illinois, in 1922, when I could have been born in the mountains of Northern Iraq where my father was a shepherd?"

As you can imagine, life in Iraq as a shepherd was extremely difficult for my father, Avrahim (Abraham).

My dad left his hometown of Asheta about 1910, before World War I, and travelled through Persia, Russia (now called the Commonwealth of Independent States), Germany and Poland, arriving in the United States about 1912. His father was a priest in the Church of the East. His family is known as the family of priests. It looks like the sons are maintaining that tradition through the sovereignty of

God. He settled in Chicago, where he soon discovered there was not much of a job opportunity for shepherds (but, praise God, thanks to His heavenly hand, today, I am a shepherd of a spiritual flock)!

My mother (her father was a deacon in the Nestorian Church) journeyed to America because of a persecution that broke out. Her village was Zarni which was north of the former capital of Assyria, Nineveh, which is presently named "Mosul" in Iraq.

Let me share with you a bit of that history.

When Assyria lost its land, the Assyrians settled mostly in what is now known as Northern Iraq.

During World War I, the nations which were united against Germany and Turkey were the United States, Great Britain, and others. Here are some verses from one of their war songs at that time by Shamasha Ephraim of Van.

> *Forth we go to battle, ranging o'er the mountains;*
> *Hearts all yearning forward to Mosul's fertile plains.*
> *Nineveh's fair city summons back her children.*
> *Forth we go to battle in thy name, O Mar Shimun (their spiritual leader).*

> *On the Tigris' banks lies Nineveh the holy;*
> *Her old walls shall be to us a diadem and crown.*
> *There alone, Assyrians, can our race be established.*
> *Forth we go to battle in thy name, O Mar Shimun.*

*Hark, our Nation calls - our great
Assyrian Mother;*
*Hark, young men, she calls you -
calls each one of you by name.*
*Blest that youth for ever who will hear
her calling.*
*Forth we go to battle in thy name, O
Mar Shimun.*

Now, the Assyrians were right up there in
Northern Iraq; there were many of them inside the
Turkish border. The British asked the Assyrians if
they would not consider holding that region for the
Allies.

The Assyrians agreed.

The British armed them, and the Assyrians
fought and held the Middle East for the Allies; they
were promised by the British Government that they
would have their own land after the fighting was over
(of course, that is what the Assyrians had been
desiring).

When the war ended, instead of the British
keeping their promise, they gave the land promised
to the Assyrians to the Moslem Arabs!

Turkey, when attacked by the Christian states of
Europe, took the war to be a kind of "jihad" (holy
war) against the Christian "infidels."

Soon, friction erupted between the Turkish
authorities and their Assyrian subjects, to the point
of an Assyrian uprising. A number of scholars hold
that the Russians (and probably the British, as well),
encouraged this revolt by promising the Assyrians
autonomy or full independence after the defeat of the
Turks.

It is beyond question, however, that the insurrection cost the Assyrians dearly.

Initially, they succeeded in repulsing a number of attacks by government forces assisted by units of Kurds (who had been the Assyrians' sworn enemies since time immemorial).

But soon afterward, they found themselves under siege and had to fight their way out to move their entire community - from infants to the elderly, a total of some seventy-thousand souls - through sub-zero weather over snow-covered mountains to Iran.

For a while thereafter, they enjoyed the patronage of the Russians, who provided them with weapons for self-defense.

With Russia's withdrawal from the war (following the Bolshevik Revolution) and the subsequent stabilization of British rule in Iraq, His Majesty's Government extended its protection to the Assyrians and brought to Iraq those who had survived the sword, disease, the hardships of exile, and their journey - altogether their numbers were reduced to some thirty-five to forty thousand people.

Then, the British recruited fighting units among the Assyrians, using them to squash sporadic rebellions within the country and in border clashes with the Turks. Taking full advantage of the Assyrians' loyalty and eagerness to please, they also cultivated the illusion of a "common fate," and went so far as to dub the Assyrians "our smallest ally" - an expression that bespoke both affection and contempt.

Further, the British continually nurtured their ally's hopes of settling in the mountainous region of northern Iraq, where they felt at home.

Such illusions were shattered one after another as the British mandate drew to a close.

For although the Anglo-Iraqi Pact of 1930 referred to the status of the various minorities in Iraq, including the Assyrians, when the mandate came to an end, the Assyrians found that all they had to show for their loyalty were vague and empty promises - and **no tangible territory**.

Worse yet, when they realized they were unwelcome in independent Iraq, some tried to return to Turkey; the Turks greeted them with machine-gun fire.

When they tried to enter Syria - in the hope that the French mandatory authorities would allow them to settle in the country's broad plain in the north - they were turned back at the border.

That is why a wave of Assyrians came to America after World War I, most making it to Chicago, where the nation's largest Assyrian population now thrives.

The Assyrians, it should be noted, are all professing Christians.

There is not a Moslem among them!

You could put a gun to an Assyrian's head and say, "Now, you must change from Christianity to the Moslem faith, or we will kill you," and each Assyrian would answer, "Kill me, I'll never do it."

That is how strong the Assyrians are for Christianity.

Today, there are about 3,000,000 Christian Assyrians living in the Middle East!

Most of the Assyrians were left in Northern Iraq, exposed to the wrath of the Turks under whom they were ruled. For over four-hundred years, in the

Ottoman Empire, all that region was under the Turks, including the Assyrians.

Can you imagine how the Turks felt since they are Moslems and the Assyrians are Christians?

The Assyrians had fought on the side of the Allies, and now, here are the Assyrians left holding an empty bag of false promises, and the Turks and the Kurds, who are also Moslem, turned on the Assyrians and massacred thousands of them.

The Assyrians had to flee.

My mother was one of those who had to flee into Iran (known as Persia in those days).

My mother fled to Persia, and while there she went to a Presbyterian school for girls, where she became a teacher and became "born again."

Then, in 1920, she came over to the United States, and that is where she met my father.

They were married in Chicago in 1921, where I was born in 1922, and raised with my family, ultimately consisting of my brothers, Benjamin, George and Joseph, and my sister, Bertha.

The first language I spoke as a child was Assyrian, since my father could not speak English. My mother taught me English to prepare me for kindergarten.

I remember how Assyrians living in the near north side of Chicago would gather together in Lincoln Park on Sundays after church to share their stories, tea and Khada (a flat bread with butter and flour filling) and the delicious Dolma (grape leaves stuffed with rice, lamb and spices).

They all spoke in Assyrian, but we children stuck with English because we did not want to seem like foreigners.

Right now, there are about 70,000 Assyrians in Chicago, but many of them have been going to California, and one of the largest Assyrian populations in the United States is in Los Angeles, California. Assyrians like California because the temperature and weather are similar to that in Iraq.

My mother was a godly woman.

My father was not too close to the Lord at first. He prided himself in the fact that his background was the Ancient Apostolic Church of the East, and my mother went to an Assyrian Presbyterian Church in Chicago.

There are now about ten Assyrian churches in Chicago, including an Assyrian Pentecostal church. Later on, my father started attending the Assyrian Pentecostal Church where he became born-again.

My mother was a prayer warrior.

Oh, could she pray!

I was the oldest of the five children. I went to Sunday School at the Presbyterian church until I was about twelve; after twelve, I quit going to church.

My father could not get a job in Chicago as a shepherd, so he worked in one of the downtown hotels as a cook.

And then the Depression hit!

Like so many others, we were poor, and I quit going to Sunday school and started selling newspapers on Sunday. I would get an armful of papers in a little wagon, then go through the streets shouting, "Get your morning newspaper here."

I guess I was getting trained for preaching later on, because I would shout, "Get your morning newspaper!" very early and very loud each morning.

Some would purchase a paper; some would tell me to shut up.

Then, with the little money I had as a youngster, I would gamble; I hate to admit it, but I just fell into the ways of the world (not being saved at the time).

I quit going to Sunday school, and did not step inside of a church again from the time I was twelve until I personally received the Lord while serving in the Navy when I was twenty.

During that time, my mother was heart-broken to see her son floundering in the ways of the world; after all, she had dedicated her first-born son to God! I was dedicated to God, but here I was going the way of the world. All of my other brothers and sister were saved, so I was like the spiritually stubborn black sheep of the family.

I secured a job working for a dentist when I was about fourteen. My biggest responsibility was going to a "bookie joint" to place bets for this dentist, then wait there until I found out if the horse won or not, then come back with the money, or tell him the horse lost.

That is the kind of environment I lived in.

My mother tried to talk to me about the Lord, and those conversations deteriorated to the point where I finally said, "I do not want to hear anything anymore about religion and God."

Truthfully, I was so convicted about being saved when she talked about God that I felt uncomfortable and wanted her to stop. She had taught me when I was a little fellow about the Lord, but now that I was "older," I wanted no part of God.

When I was younger, she would often sink to her knees, look me in the eyes, and teach me about Jesus. Then, she would question me to see how much I absorbed from her teaching and from the Word of God.

But as I grew older, I drifted away from religion, saying, "I do not want to hear about it."

Mother respected my wishes and stopped sharing about God; she knew I would become upset and run out of the house if she started sharing scripture with me.

So, she prayed.

She would go into her prayer closet and sometimes I would even hear her praying.

As a teenager, when I came home late at night after living a rowdy life, I would go to bed only to be awakened in the middle of the night.

There would be my mother at my bedside, praying.

She would just slip in and pray over me.

Mothers, be faithful in your prayers!

Your child can never get away from those prayers.

As you persist, God will honor your heart and your children will come to the Lord. They will eventually be won into the Kingdom of God.

In truth, I was the most unlikely one to be saved.

But when I was in the Navy during World War II, I started to think, "What if I died, what is going to happen to me?"

I knew from my mother's teaching that I would go to hell if I died, so I reasoned, "Now, is it worth it to live my life the way I am living it and die and go to hell for all eternity?"

Fortunately, I said "No."

I loved to gamble, and God used that gambling instinct in me to bring me to my conversion. No one talked to me specifically about the Lord; it was just through my mother's teachings and prayers that I came to the Lord.

When I went into the war, I was not thinking at the time that there was a heaven or a hell. Instead, I was trying to believe that "There is no God" so I would not be convicted.

But in the face of war, my thoughts went another direction.

I reasoned, "If I live to be seventy, and suppose there is a heaven and hell, if I keep living the way I am living now, I will be in hell forever.

"But, if I accept the Lord and live a good life, and if there is no heaven or hell, I have not lost anything; I have just lived a good life."

So, I concluded, "What is keeping me from accepting the Lord?"

I thought deeply about the junk I was doing, and I said to myself, "I am throwing away eternity for this junk? No, I do not want to die and go to hell."

As a gambler, I did not like the odds: Seventy years of dubious fun verses eternity.

I remembered my mom teaching about accepting Christ, so I prayed, "Lord, I want to accept You as my personal savior, I want to be saved. Please enter into my heart today. I ask Your forgiveness for my sins, and ask You to accept me into Your spiritual family, and change my life. Amen."

When I said that simple prayer, a huge, invisible weight seemed to be removed from my heart! Immediately I shouted, "Praise God, this is just the peaceful feeling I have been looking for in the world."

An unexplainable joy came to me.

I started reading the New Testament (the Gideon organization had given each of us servicemen a New Testament). I started reading about how Jesus died for my sins, and my heart was broken.

> *"For God so loved the world, that he gave his only begotten Son, that whosoever believeth in him should not perish, but have everlasting life" (John 3:16).*

I had originally accepted Jesus Christ because I was afraid of hell.

But now, as I read about Jesus dying for me, I fell in love with Him, and my heart just broke. I wept, "O Jesus, You did all of this for me? You gave up Your life so that I might spend eternity with You in heaven? Thank You, Lord Jesus. Now, I am going to live the rest of my life for You."

Then, I started witnessing to my Navy buddies.

I would say, "Hey, you know this being a Christian is great! I used to think if you became a Christian, you would not have any fun; I was all prepared when I accepted Christ not to have any fun. I was among some people who said 'You cannot do this, you cannot do that,' and I thought 'Man, it is no fun being a Christian'."

But I was wrong.

"Hey, this is the greatest joy; there is nothing in the world so empty as when I go to the taverns, laugh with the boys, and then go home and feel so lonesome, so empty."

It seemed as though my worldly life in the Navy had given me nothing.

I was so excited about the changes God was doing in my life that I called up mother and told her, "I just accepted Jesus Christ as my Lord and Savior."

You can well imagine how my mother rejoiced when she heard the news!

Her consistent and persistent prayers had been answered!

"The effectual fervent prayer of a righteous man avails much" (James 5:16).

My mother already knew in her spirit that I was going to be in the ministry (that is a story for my next book). God led me through the Navy, Navigators, memorizing the Word, etc., and then ultimately, He called me into the ministry, where my mother lived to see me ordained.

Eventually, I studied at the Moody Bible Institute Night School, then enrolled in Northern Baptist Theological Seminary in Chicago in 1946, graduating in 1950 with a Bachelor of Theology degree.

During this time, while attending and serving in my home church, Moody Memorial in Chicago, I met my lovely wife, Burnell Hanson who had also begun attending the church. She had come from Wakerfield, Michigan, to train at the Augustana Hospital School of Nursing. After graduating as a Registered Nurse, she was employed as a floor supervisor in the hospital. We were engaged in March, 1947, and were married in her home town in June, 1948.

Next, I went to Northwestern University Graduate School in Evanston, Illinois, where I received a Master of Arts degree in the School of Speech.

Here is an interesting point.

My mother was the first intercessor I ever knew.

Today, I am exceedingly blessed to be able to represent Intercessors for America - a national organization that recognizes the power of prayer, and petitions its members each month to pray and fast for various pressing needs in our nation.

How mother must be rejoicing and praising God in heaven today for the power of prayer that changed her son's life, and for the power of prayer her son is now using to transform individual lives, and to change the course of nations (later I will share my exciting meetings with the Prime Minister of Israel, Menachem Begin, and at a separate time, with Egyptian President Hosni Mubarak)!

CHAPTER ONE

THE ASSYRIA/ISRAEL CONNECTION

This book is going to take you on an adventure into biblical prophecy - where you will discover exciting endtime events concerning the forgotten nation in prophecy - Assyria.

Some Christians confuse Assyria with "Syria;" they are not the same. Put an "As" in front of "Syria" and you have "Assyria." Syria is a country that exists today, but there is no country today currently called "Assyria."

That nation - not the people - has vanished from current maps on geography.

Yet today, **there are almost four million Assyrians living all across our globe!**

Assyria was a once-powerful nation mentioned over 150 times in the Bible, yet today, when so much is being written about endtime Israel and the role of the Jew, Assyria has become the forgotten nation in prophecy.

It may seem strange to you to be reading a book about a nation that does not currently have a homeland.

Assyrians are living all around the globe, but like the Jews in the early 1940's, they do not YET have a new homeland to call their own.

Currently, they reside mainly in Iraq, Syria, and the United States (see appendix in the back of this book for a fairly complete breakdown of the Assyrian population around the globe and in the United States).

You may wonder... "If Assyrians are scattered around the world, and if there is no longer a nation called `Assyria', then why write a book about Assyria?"

Because, in this endtime hour, I believe the Bible clearly declares through prophecy that...

THE ASSYRIANS WILL ONCE AGAIN BE GIVEN THEIR OWN HOMELAND BY GOD!

That action is not unprecedented.

The Jews wandered the earth without a homeland until Israel was miraculously born again on May 14, 1948, when a Jew named David Ben-Gurion (the first Prime Minister of Israel, who wrote in his memoirs, "Our ancestors, the Assyrians") declared:

> "By virtue of the natural and historical right of the Jewish people and the Resolution of the General Assembly of the United Nations, we hereby proclaim the establishment of the Jewish state in Palestine to be called ISRAEL..."

After that declaration, two million Jews from all over the world started returning to the Holy Land. The event marked one of the greatest miracles in history, and also was the fulfillment of an endtime prophecy:

> "For I will take you from among the heathen, and gather you out of all countries, and will bring you into your own land" (Ezekiel 36:24).

The re-establishment of Israel also fulfilled another prophecy:

> *"Who hath heard such a thing? Who hath seen such things? Shall the earth be made to bring forth in one day? or shall a nation be born at once? for as soon as Zion travailed, she brought forth her children" (Isaiah 66:8).*

I believe a similar miraculous fate awaits the Assyrian people.

In this book, I will show that one of the endtime signs Christians should be watching for is the <u>re-establishment of Assyria as a nation!</u>

The area once called Assyria and, I believe, soon to be called Assyria again, is roughly the geography of Syria, Iraq, Iran, and part of Turkey, with most of it occupying Iraq.

But today, as you hold this book in your hands, Assyria is an invisible country. It does not exist.

This fact has deep emotional concerns for me because I am an Assyrian American. My ancestors were from the rich and powerful land of Mesopotamia (Assyria) which lies between the Tigris and the Euphrates Rivers, just north of the Garden of Eden.

Today, this entire area, once called "The Crescent of Civilization," is now Iran and Iraq (see appendix for a map of ancient Assyria).

As you read this book, you will discover many biblical and historical surprises about Assyria.

One fact that often shocks Christians the most is this - **<u>Assyrians</u> living throughout the world are** not Arabs or Moslems by religion - we <u>are</u> <u>Christians</u>!

* **Jesus grew up with Assyrians:**

As the Old Testament is the heritage of the Jewish people, the New Testament is the heritage of the Assyrians! Their Gospel text dates from the second century, nearly two hundred years closer to Christ than the Greek manuscript. Jesus Christ was reared in Nazareth of Galilee; Galilee was mostly of Assyrian lineage. Jesus was reared amongst Assyrians and spoke Assyrian (Aramaic).

* **Jesus preached in Assyrian**:

That was the language of the people where He lived. All the apostles spoke and wrote in Aramaic.

King Abgar, the Assyrian king, was the first king who appreciated and understood Christ (according to Assyrian Church history). He invited Christ to his kingdom saying, "My kingdom is enough for you and me." Jesus ordered one of his disciples to go to the King (said to be Thomas) and cure him of his disease and preach to his people the message of Christianity.

* **The Assyrians were the first to accept Christianity.**

It was in the second year after the Ascension of Christ that Christianity showed its first signs in Mesopotamia. About this time, Thomas was one of the twelve who had begun the preaching and teaching of the Gospel and the new religion, which was prophetically destined to embrace all of Beth-Nahrain, "the land of two rivers" (later called Iraq).

Mar Toma, as Thomas was called, was the first missionary to the Assyrians. He continued with his apostolic mission until 45 A.D., twelve years after the Ascension, and he proceeded to India to begin his pioneering activities in Christian teaching there. The results of his work still exists in Malabar, India, under the present Archbishop Mar Temateuss (Assyrian).

In the meantime, Mar Shimon Patros (Simon called Peter) had succeeded Thomas as the apostle to Mesopotamia. It was during this tenure of apostolic mission that the first Christian church was founded in Babylon, thus establishing the Eastern church.

> *"The church that is at Babylon, elected together with you, saluteth you; and so doth Marcos my son" (I Peter 5:13).*

* Books of the New Testament were first written in Assyrian (Aramaic) as Christ spoke it.

Nearly all Biblical names derive their meanings from Aramaic. Assyrian continued to be the colloquial and literary language of the Jews until the ninth century. See pages 119, 120 for Aramaic words that appear in the Bible.

* Assyrians carried the message of Christ to remote corners of the World such as Tibet, Mongolia, China, Japan, Indonesia and Ethiopia.

The Assyrian Church, or as it is now known, the Ancient Apostolic Church of the East, was one of the strongest Christian Churches in the world, and was noted for its missions in the Middle East, India, China, Mongolia, Indonesia, Japan and other parts of the world.

* The oldest Christian Church in the World is the Assyrian Church of Mart Mariam of Urumia in Northwest Iran.

Reportedly, the Church of Mart Mariam was established by the three wise Kings of the East who followed the bright star in the East to the place of Jesus' birth - where they worshipped Him.

* An Assyrian (Aramaic) New Testament, written by hand on vellum, was perhaps the oldest New Testament in the world.

Assyrians were and are staunch Christians. Even while fighting as soldiers, they used to fast for the Lenten season and abide by other church holidays. During this fast, they would abstain not only from meat, but from everything that was animal, including milk, fish, butter and eggs.

Today, Assyrians still speak our ancient mother tongue, Aramaic, the language of Christ! (Today in our homes we speak modern Aramaic which is called "Syriac".)

The Assyrians have a long and proud heritage of contributions that they have given to Western civilization (more about this later in the book) - FAR MORE than most people can ever begin to realize.

Assyrians played an important part in the history of the Near East, of the Bible, and of world religion in general.

The ancient city of Nineveh was converted to the Lord by Jonah. The destruction of Nineveh in 612 B.C. scattered the Assyrians all over the world, but most Assyrians still live in the Middle Eastern countries.

Presently, there are about 300,000 Assyrians living in the United States, and over one and one-half million in Iraq.

We have upheld all of our traditions and customs, and still speak our ancient mother tongue. Even though we do not have a country anymore, we have survived steadfastly through the centuries.

In this book, I will share with you some of the rich history of the Assyrians, which can be found throughout the Old Testament of the Bible, and also reveal to you some **SHOCKING TRUTHS concerning endtime biblical prophecy and the nation of Assyria**!

People think we do not exist anymore because we do not have a country.

This book will show you conclusively that we are alive, well, united and anxious to see what God is going to do in this endtime hour to restore our nation!

We are looking forward to once again having our own country!

The Jews received their newly formed nation of Israel on May 14, 1948.

And God's Word guarantees that BEFORE the endtime hour of spiritual history comes to pass, Assyria will once again have their own country!

As you shall see later in this book, that statement is not based upon the fond hopes of one Assyrian, but upon a clear, firm biblical promise!

Throughout the ages, God has used Assyria.

In this endtime hour, we have HIS Word that He will once again use Assyria for His glory!

Look at Isaiah 10:5:

> *"O Assyrian, the rod of mine anger, and the staff in their hand is mine indignation."*

"Woe to the Assyrians," God said, "the rod of my anger in whose hand is the club of my wrath." God used Assyria as His club of wrath and judgement upon His people, Israel, who had backslidden and forsaken Him. Assyria was the second world kingdom to oppress Israel - the first was Egypt.

The fact that God has used both Assyria and Egypt to chastise Israel will become an extremely important point as this book develops!

Assyria and Israel are closely connected through almost all of scripture. The words "Assyria" and "Assyrian" are found in the Bible 151 times, and in nearly every case they are in connection with Israel.

God directs the great Assyrian armies against many foes, and they are invincible. The Assyrians are used to capture and enslave the Israelites because they turned from Him and worshipped idols.

> *"I will send him against an hypocritical nation, and against the people of my wrath will I give him a charge, to take the spoil, and to take the prey, and to tread them down like the mire of the streets" (Isaiah 10:6).*

I believe today that in the ancient land of Assyria (now called Iraq), God is using Iraq as a rod of His anger upon Israel.

After all, the scud missiles which were dropped on Israel certainly created woes.

When the patterns of war started to emerge, I could not believe Saddam Hussein would dare to take on the whole world.

But, when the Gulf War broke out, he tried.

It almost seemed as if it were a sovereign plan pushing him blindly forward.

Nothing else makes much sense.

But when he kept the invasion into Kuwait and took on the whole United Nations coalition, including the United States with all its military power, the Assyrian Democratic Movement, the Assyrian Universal Alliance, Bet-Nahrin Democratic Party, and the Assyrian Democratic Organization, all called for the withdrawal of Iraqi forces from Kuwait. (In an advertisement page in *The New York Times*).

But God was using Iraq as He did Assyria in the Old Testament - as a rod of His anger to chastise, to bring people around to God.

Have you ever noticed how world conflict and crisis always brings people around to God?

Look how much prayer was going on when President Bush called for a National Day of Prayer for the Gulf War. We already have an annual National Day of Prayer, but we hardly hear anything about it. It is always on the first Thursday in May.

But during the conflict with Iraq, when the President called for a National Day of Prayer, even the secular media reported on it, reminding us to pray!

According to the reports from the various Christian chaplains, thousands of young soldiers stationed in the Gulf came to know the Lord through their duties in Saudi Arabia.

God used that Gulf War and that time to bring many new lost souls into His spiritual family.

As the endtime hour increases, I believe God will continue to use that part of our globe, the Middle East, in ever-increasing intensity, as a tool to reach lost souls with the message of Jesus Christ before the entire endtime scenario is finally played out here on Earth.

AN ASSYRIAN/ISRAELI MEETING TAKES PLACE

In 1992, a cordial conversation was held between Dr. Yitzchzk Ben-Gad, Consul-General of the State of Israel and Assyrians of Chicago in Consul Ben-Gad's office in Chicago. Some of the impressions and comments made by Dr. Ben-Gad follow:

"Assyrians have a magnificent history, culture and civilization. They had many kingdoms and monarches before 612 B.C. in Mesopotamia [Today northern Iraq]. Assyrian Kings like Sargon built cities, constructed aqueducts, established a system of government and an urban and urbane life. King Ashurbanipal built the first library. Today, the Iraqi government of Saddam Hussein wants to eradicate all that and wipe it off history books.

Assyrians and Jews are nephews with a common forefather - Abraham. Abraham left the Ur of Chaldae c.2,000 B.C. Ur then located in southern Assyrian [today near Basra in southern Iraq]. He migrated to Canaan, the Promised Land of Israel, and started the 12 tribes of Israel.

The 4 1/2 million Jews in Israel and 1 1/2 million Assyrians in Iraq share a common fate, common destiny. The 6 million Jews and Assyrians are two besieged ethnic Semitic minorities, their existence and national identities threatened by 156 million supposedly Semitic Arabs.

The languages of Assyrians and Jews have a common origin. Aramaic and Hebrew are cognate languages with common vocabularies. Cognate words include: Shalom=Shlama (peace); Shabat=Shabta (Saturday); Alohim=Alaha (God); Rabbi=Rabi (teachers,priest); Nisan=Nisan (April); Tamus=Tmas (July); Tishirn=Tishirn (October); Tahneen=Taneena (alligator)...." (From *The Assyrian Guardian*, September, 1992).

CHAPTER TWO

THE INVENTIVE IMAGINATIONS
OF THE EARLY ASSYRIANS!

To understand how God is going to use Assyria in this endtime hour, and to understand the full impact of "THE HIDDEN SCRIPTURE" I referred to in the Introduction, it is first important for you to have a basic understanding of how God has used Assyria throughout the ages. The first time Assyria is mentioned in the Old Testament is in Genesis 2: 14:

> *"And the name of the third river is Hiddekel: that is it, which goeth toward the east of Assyria. And the fourth river is Euphrates."*

The "Hiddekel" river is the "TIGRIS" river. The Euphrates river is the river Abraham crossed over when he left Ur of the Chaldees with his father, Terah (Genesis 11:31), and had settled in Haran (between the two rivers Tigris and Euphrates, in Northwest Mesopotamia).

Abraham left Haran and crossed over the Euphrates River on his way to Canaan in obedience to God. The Aramaic word "Habar" means "to cross over" from which we get the word "Hebrew". Abraham, the Assyrian, is the father of both Jews and Arabs through his sons Isaac and Ishmael. And through Abraham God promised that all families of the earth would be blessed (Genesis 12:3).

The Tigris is the river which flows east of Assyria. The fourth river is the Euphrates.

You can always identify old Assyria because it was between the two rivers, the Euphrates and Tigris.

Then look at Genesis 2:10:

> "And a river went out of Eden to water the garden; and from thence it was parted, and became into four heads."

Assyria is where the Garden of Eden was located! It was in the southern part of Assyria.

Bordering Assyria, then, were four rivers, two of them being the Tigris and Euphrates.

The Assyrian empire was founded by Asshur, the son of Shem. The Semitic people came from Shem, the people of the Middle East.

> "Out of that land went forth Asshur, and builded Nineveh, and the city Rehoboth, and Calah,
> "And Resen between Nineveh and Calah: the same is a great city" (Genesis 10:11-12).

The early Assyrians made so many contributions to our current culture that it is almost impossible to document all that they have done. In the following few pages, I will chronicle just some of their major achievements.

THOSE AMAZING, INVENTIVE ASSYRIANS!

It is hard to imagine what our lives would be like today without the contributions of the Assyrians, known as the people from Mesopotamia, **the cradle of civilization**, in Southwest Asia. They are an extension of the Babylonian heritage, and are the root of our modern, western civilization.

The Assyrians, 4000 years ago, **invented glass** by experimenting with sand and quartz, and ultimately, were responsible for the concept of **glass lenses**. These early discoveries were the forerunners to the eyeglasses many of you are using today to read this book. They took these concepts to also invent the first magnifying glass.

Assyrians were the first inventors, developing such important contributions as **crystal, glazed brick and stained glass.**

And what would our world be like today if there were no laws, no system of justice?

The Assyrians **formed and enacted laws and government.** The first systematically collected and enacted set of laws was during the reign of King Hammurabi, who ruled 4000 years ago in Babylon. I would dare say most students of history have heard of the **Code of Hammurabi.**

The Code of Hammurabi consisted of **282 codes**; economic provisions were made for prices, tariffs, trade and commerce; family law, marriage and divorce; criminal law, assault and theft. Even civil law, which covered slavery and death, was a part of the code.

Penalties varied according to the status of the offenders and the circumstances of the offenses.

These laws were written in **Cuneiform**, or wedge-shaped characters, rather than pictorial characters, foreshadowing the arrival of **the alphabetic script** now used throughout much of the world.

In Mesopotamia, 5000 years ago, a practical system of **writing** was developed, bringing about a revolution in communications.

Writing is so much a part of our lives today that it would be hard to imagine our world without it. You could not be holding this book in your hands today without the Assyrian contribution to writing.

Further, the accumulation of knowledge through writing gave way to **the first library**, in Nineveh, the capital city of the Assyrian empire, during the Kingdom of Asshurbanipal, around the 7th century B.C. This library, preserved in clay tablets, contains a large number of historical narratives and ancient legends.

Among the tablets is "The Epic of Gilgamish," an early account of the story of the flood.

The library also holds many documents on science, astronomy and natural history. These documents were arranged systemically on shelves, and special indications helped the reader to locate them.

The preservation of knowledge through writing created **the first academic centers** of learning. Scribes began to specialize in teaching on specific subjects such as science and language - even the construction of houses, temples, and ships.

Mathematics played an important part in the Assyrian culture. You may have learned Roman Numerals when you were a small child, but they were not practical for solving a complicated math problem; they are cumbersome and confusing to employ.

Our system of **modern mathematics** comes from the Assyrians and the Babylonians. This mathematic method is based on indicating the value of a number by its relative position.

In comparison, the Egyptian method, the Roman numeral system designed 2000 years later, is only able to handle a simple linear equation.

The Babylonian system of mathematics was first developed in Mesopotamia, and is still used internationally. These mathematical developments have served to bring progress in other areas.

Our modern lives are structured around the concept of **time.**

Can you imagine going from place to place without the awareness of time in our daily schedules?

The Babylonians were the ones who first learned how to **measure time** by dividing the day into twenty-four hours, and then the hour into sixty minutes, and then the minute into sixty seconds.

They also divided the year into twelve months, and devised a seven day week in honor of the seven planets (the only planets they knew about at the time). They were also the first to divide a circle into 360 degrees, and used this knowledge to help evolve the first **arcs** used in architecture and building.

Mesopotamia is where the first known **wheeled vehicle** was made. This discovery revolutionized the world's system of transportation, and introduced the wheeled vehicle - <u>**probably the greatest and most revolutionary mechanical invention of all time**</u> - to the world!

The Mesopotamian contribution to **musical notation** and musical theory has just recently been discovered. Archaeologists have known for many years that Mesopotamians had musical instruments, particularly harps and lyres.

But, it was only recently when a Cuneiform tablet that had mystified scholars for seventy years was interpreted that the history of music and musical theory was carried back more than one thousand years before the first known Greek musical notation!

Before that time, it was generally believed that music was no older than the European middle ages. This new discovery verifies the first record in history of a **musical scale** and a coherent musical system.

They also introduced musical poetry, the root of our modern day songs.

The people from Mesopotamia invented many techniques and tools for our Western civilization which have never changed in their basic designs.

They were also responsible for **the first cities**, and gave birth to the development of **city planning**. They constructed many multi-story towers, including the tower of Babel.

They are also responsible for the magnificent hanging gardens of Babylon, and originated the construction of huge bridges, canals and aqueducts, and efficient sewage disposal systems.

The Assyrians created incredible architectural designs, such as the Gate of Ishtar.

Further, they developed the use of **metal**, generated the advancement of **astronomy**, and developed the **first observatory**, calculating the movement of the planets, forecasting the eclipse of the moon, and creating the twelve signs of the zodiac.

They birthed art in visual animal pictures and pottery, perfected sailing ships, and founded agriculture, bringing man to the end of his nomadic existence.

They invented **the plow**, creating the first economic revolution.

They developed **irrigation**, bringing large areas of land under cultivation by watering them artificially.

They developed a merchant class and a **system of trade**.

They manufactured **linen**, creating the textile industry.

And finally, perhaps the most shocking and unknown discovery of all attributed to the Assyrians, they were **the first men to travel by air without the aid of any machines!!!**

There was a fascinating division in the Assyrian Empire called "Tiarayee," and they had the responsibility to scout and observe the enemy in war, observing fortifications and locating the movements and detachments of the enemy.

To accomplish this goal, they had stables of trained eagles to carry their soldiers. Here is how the Assyrian "Air Force" worked.

Before the eagles were put in flight, they were kept indoors blindfolded and without food for two or three days. When the eagles became very hungry, they were attached to a strong woven basket suitable to accommodate people. The basket was fixed at the end of a long pole, while the other end was tied to the jackets which were fastened around the body of the eagles (similar to a horse and carriage).

A pilot and an observer would then sit tightly in the basket (usually these were young, lightweight boys). The pilot would carry a long cane pointing high up in the sky. At the tip of the cane there was a hook and a bait of fresh meat.

At this point, the ground staff would unfold the eyes of the four eagles attached to the basket, and by the sight of the bait high above their heads, the starving eagles, quite familiar with the exercise, would take off and fly to get at the bait, thus lifting the basket and the young men inside it high up into the air!

The adjustment of the basket in flight was made by the pilot, varying the altitude and the latitude in accordance with the raising and the lowering of the pole on which the bait was fixed. The observers could now fly above the enemy territories observing their strength, defense positions and military installations.

On completion of the mission, the pilot would lower the bait-pole in a descending position until the basket reached the ground. Then, the eagles were groomed by the ground staff and fed with chunks of meat. (Believe it or not!).

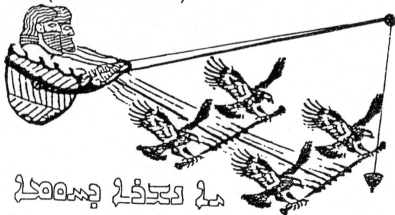

I discovered this picture of the Assyrian eagle air patrol at the British Museum in London.

As we chart our endtime destiny on the planet earth, we must remember these major contributions of the Assyrians to our world-wide community.

The generations of people from Mesopotamia have left a significant legacy to our generation - a legacy seldom fully understood or appreciated by most of our current culture.

I sincerely hope this chapter has heightened your awareness of the major contributions of the Assyrian people to our modern-day culture, and helps you appreciate the brilliance and inventiveness of this forgotten nation called by historians the "Cradle of Civilization"!

CHAPTER THREE

THE BIBLICAL BACKGROUND
OF THE ASSYRIANS

The Assyrians of today are descendants of the ancient Assyrian people who played a major role in the foundation of the world's civilization.

Their ancient homeland was Mesopotamia (today called Iraq).

The first biblical mention of this ancient people is contained in Genesis 10:10-12:

> *"And the beginning of his kingdom was Babel, and Erech, and Accad, and Calneh, in the land of Shinar.*
> *"Out of that land went forth Asshur, and builded Nineveh, and the city Rehoboth, and Calah,*
> *"And Resen between Nineveh and Calah: the same is a great city."*

Look how early this is in the history of the world in the Bible (Assyria is estimated to have been established about 3000 years before Christ).

From the land of Shinar, Asshur went forth and built Nineveh, the capital city of Assyria (ultimately destroyed in 612 BC).

Later, in Genesis 10:22, we read:

"The children of Shem; Elam, and Asshur, and Arphax-ad, and Lud, and Aram" (Genesis 10:22).

Asshur was one of the children of Shem; God used Asshur to found Nineveh, the Capital city of the nation of Assyria. Because Asshur was the founder, the early pronunciation for our people was Asshurian (when I ministered in the Middle East, the people there still referred to me as an Asshurian - in honor of Asshur, the founder of Assyria).

Then, in 2 Kings 17, the next significant mention of the Assyrian nation relates to Israel (as you will soon discover, Assyria and Israel are closely related throughout the entire Bible in their histories and influence upon each other):

"Against him came up Shalmaneser king of Assyria; and Hoshea became his servant, and gave him presents" (II Kings 17:3).

Shalmaneser, the king of Assyria, decided to attack Hoshea, the king of Israel, in Samaria. At the time, Samaria consisted of the ten tribes of Israel. The original twelve-tribe kingdom had been divided into the Northern and the Southern regions.

The Northern kingdom, composed of the ten tribes of Israel, was called Samaria.

The two remaining tribes comprised the Southern kingdom, called Judea.

So Shalmaneser came against Samaria, the Northern kingdom, for failing to pay proper tribute (as had been done in previous years). As part of this process (all documented in II Kings 17), the king of

Assyria confirmed Hoshea was the main traitor who had stopped paying proper tribute to him.

Therefore, Shalmaneser put him into prison.

But the battle in Samaria was not a quick one.

The king of Assyria invaded the land, marched against all of Samaria, besieged it for three years, and in the <u>ninth year</u> of Hoshea, **Shalmaneser captured Samaria and <u>deported</u> the Israelites to Assyria.**

Now look what happens!

The king of Assyria imported all the inhabitants of the ten tribes of Israel to Assyria, including the nobles and all the upperclass. He settled them in Halah and in Harbor by the river of Gozan, and in the cities of the Medes (II Kings 17:6).

This is the very beginning of the dispersment of the Israelites that is foretold in scripture!

> *"And the LORD shall scatter you among the nations, and ye shall be left few in number among the heathen, whither the LORD shall lead you" (Deuteronomy 4:27).*

Throughout the course of this book, you will discover that God uses Assyria throughout the Bible to influence the Jews and the nation of Israel.

And, in this endtime hour of history, God is going to use these two nations together again (even though Assyria does not exist as a nation as you read this book)!

Now, let us look at verses 23 and 24.

> *"Until the LORD removed Israel out of his sight, as he had said by all his servants the prophets. So was Israel*

carried away out of their own land to Assyria unto this day.

"And the king of Assyria brought men from Babylon, and from Cuthah, and from Ava, and from Hamath, and from Sepharvaim, and placed them in the cities of Samaria instead of the children of Israel: and they possessed Samaria, and dwelt in the cities thereof."

The people of Israel were taken from their homeland into exile in Assyria, and many of them are still there today. That is why **the ten tribes of Israel all spoke Assyrian** - because they were taken to Assyria. This was the start of the dispersion of the Jews, according to the Scripture:

"And they shall fall by the edge of the sword, and shall be led away captive into all nations:" (Luke 21:24).

Look what else happened.

The king of Assyria brought people from Babylon, Cuthah, Ava, Hamath and Sepharvaim and settled them in the town of Samaria to replace the Israelites.

So, the king took Assyrians and put them into the cities of the Northern ten kingdoms. He literally performed a gigantic population switch, moving the Assyrians amongst the ten tribes, and moving the ten tribes (the Israelites) into Assyria.

Precisely because of this extensive intermingling, **Jesus Christ spoke Assyrian** (the Assyrian language was Aramaic).

"Wherefore they spake to the king of Assyria, saying, The nations which thou hast removed, and placed in the cities of Samaria, know not the manner of the God of the land: therefore he hath sent lions among them, and, behold, they slay them, because they know not the manner of the God of the land.

"Then the king of Assyria commanded, saying, Carry thither one of the priests whom ye brought from thence; and let them go and dwell there, and let him teach them the manner of the God of the land" (II Kings 17:26-27).

In these two verses, we see that the King of Assyria learned that the people he deported and resettled in the town of Samaria did not know what the God of that country required. As a result, God had sent lions among them to punish and kill them because of their spiritual ignorance.

So, the King of Assyria decided to give this order: "Have one of the priests you took captive from Samaria go back to live there and teach the Assyrian people what the God of the land requires."

Talk about God having a powerful evangelistic system! So, they sent a priest from the Israelite tribes to the Assyrians living in the land of Samaria so they could learn about the great God Jehovah!

From the passages we have studied thus far, you now know why Christ spoke Assyrian, and how the Assyrians were taught by the Israelites about the great God Jehovah.

However, the most important point to note is that **the Assyrians were used as God's instrument for judging His people Israel.**

God used the Assyrians to capture and enslave the Israelites because they had turned away from Him and worshipped idols.

As a result, the Jews would ultimately be scattered throughout the world and without a country until the reestablishment of Israel in May of 1948.

Now, let us shift to Isaiah 10: 5-6.

> "O Assyrian, the rod of mine anger, and the staff in their hand is mine indignation.
> "I will send him against an hypocritical nation, and against the people of my wrath will I give him a charge, to take the spoil, and to take the prey, and to tread them down like the mire of the streets."
> "Woe to the Assyrian, the rod of my anger in whose hand is the club of my wrath" (Isaiah 10:5, NIV).

Keep these scriptures tucked away in the back of your mind as we now read in Ezekiel 23; Ezekiel shows clearly how God used Assyria as His rod (Isaiah 10:5) to punish His people.

Many Christians are amazed at what this next passage reveals.

> "And Aholah (the ten tribes of Israel) played the harlot when she was mine; and she doted on her lovers, on the Assyrians her neighbors,

"Which were clothed with blue, captains and rulers, all of them desireable young men, horsemen riding upon horses.

"Thus she committed her whoredoms with them, with all them that were the chosen men of Assyria, and with all on whom she doted: with all their idols she defiled herself.

"Neither left she her whoredoms brought from Egypt: for in her youth they lay with her, and they bruised the breasts of her virginity, and poured their whoredom upon her.

"Wherefore I have delivered her into the hand of her lovers, into the hand of the Assyrians, upon whom she doted.

"These discovered her nakedness: they took her sons and her daughters, and slew her with the sword: and she became famous among women; for they had executed judgment upon her.

"And when her sister Aholibah (Jerusalem) saw this, she was more corrupt in her inordinate love than she, and in her whoredoms more than her sister in her whoredoms.

"She doted upon the Assyrians her neighbours, captains and rulers clothed most gorgeously, horsemen riding upon horses, all of them desirable young men" (Ezekiel 23:5-12).

"Aholah engaged in prostitution while she was still mine," God says.

She lusted after her lovers, the Assyrians.

She gave herself as a prostitute to the elite Assyrians - warriors clothed in blue, governors and commanders, all of the handsome young men and mounted horsemen. She defiled herself of all the idols of everyone she lusted after. She did not give up the prostitution she began in Egypt.

"Therefore, I handed her over to her lovers, the Assyrians for whom she lusted."

They stripped her naked, took away her sons and daughters, and killed her with a sword.

"Aholah" is a name for the ten tribes of Samaria; God gave that name to the Northern kingdoms.

Her sister, "Aholibah", is Jerusalem. In her lust and prostitution she was more depraved then her sister, Samaria.

The two sisters are Samaria and Jerusalem.

Jerusalem also lusted after the Assyrian governors and commanders, warriors and mounted horsemen and all handsome young men.

"Therefore, O Aholibah, thus saith the Lord God; Behold, I will raise up thy lovers against thee, from whom thy mind is alienated, and I will bring them against thee on every side;

"The Babylonians, and all the Chaldeans, Pekod, and Shoa, and Koa, and all the Assyrians with them: all of them desirable young men, captains and rulers, great lords and renowned, all of them riding upon horses.

"And they shall come against thee with chariots, wagons, and wheels, and with an assembly of people, which shall *set against thee buckler and shield and helmet round about: and I will set judgement before them, and they shall judge thee according to their judgments"* (Ezekiel 23:22-24).

"Therefore, Aholibah" (this is what the sovereign Lord says), *"I will stir up your lovers against you from every side."*

So God is telling Israel that the Babylonians and all the Chaldeans (Southern Assyrians) will come against you with weapons, chariots and wagons with strong people. He is saying, "They will take up positions against you on every side with large and small shields and with helmets. **I will turn you over to them for punishment**, and they will punish you according to their standards."

That is the rod God used against His backslidden people (Remember Isaiah 10: 5-6?).

Today, I believe a similar spiritual parallel is unfolding, and Isaiah 10 will become a reality once again.

GOD WILL USE HIS ROD AGAIN!

God will use His rod to chastise those who call themselves the people of God, like America. We call ourselves the people of God, a Christian nation, but we are not a Christian nation - morally. Of course, there are many fine Christians in this nation, but America itself is not a Christian nation any longer!

Not with 1 1/2 million abortions per year.

Not with millions of babies annually born to unwed mothers, and many of them growing up as abused children.

Not with all the major cities in this country dominated by criminals, gangs, drugs and Satanism.

Not with a BILLION DOLLAR industry in pornographic magazines and video tapes!

Not with prayer and the Bible stripped from our schools by the very Supreme Court founded to protect our right to freedom of religion!

The truth is clear - America is no longer a Christian nation, and we should do as the Assyrians in Nineveh did at the preaching of Jonah in the 8th century B.C. - repent of our sins and turn to God in humility.

I believe we will soon see the rod of God coming to chastise our nation.

This is not a message of doom and gloom.

The coming chastisement will bring about the greatest spiritual outpouring that America or the world has ever seen!

I believe that after the chastising we will see the greatest spiritual awakening ever to fall upon the entire world. For where sin increases, grace increases all the more (Romans 5:20).

Just as God has used Assyria in the past, it is a spiritual parallel that in this endtime hour God will once again use Assyria.

Just as there was a tribulation at a time of the overthrow of Jerusalem, so too there is coming another tribulation - a great tribulation.

CHAPTER FOUR

THE DECLINE OF ASSYRIAN POWER

During the reign of Hoshea, king of Israel, the Assyrian king, Shalmanseser, invaded Samaria and captured it after a siege of three years. He then deported the Israelites (the 10 tribes) to Assyria.

II Kings 17:22-23 says:

> "The Israelites persisted in all the sins of Jeroboam and did not turn away from them until the Lord removed them from his presence, as he had warned through all his servants, the prophets. So the people of Israel were taken from their homeland into exile in Assyria, and they are still there."

II Kings 18:9-12 says,

> "In King Hezekiah's fourth year, which was the seventh year of Hoshea son of Elah king of Israel, Shalmaneser king of Assyria marched against Samaria and laid siege to it. At the end of three years the Assyrians took it. So Samaria was captured in Hezekiah's sixth year, which was the ninth year of Hoshea king of Israel. The king of Assyria deported Israel to Assyria and settled them in Halah, in Gozan on the

Habor River and in towns of the Medes. This happened because they had not obeyed the Lord their God, but had violated his covenant - all that Moses the servant of the Lord commanded. They neither listened to the commands nor carried them out."

Verse 24 of Chapter 17 describes how Assyria replaced the Israelites of the ten northern tribes with Assyrians; they became the formation of the Samaritans of the New Testament as they intermarried with Israelites left in the land. Later, the Israelites who returned from the captivity in the New Testament were called "foreigners". Luke 17:18 says:

"Was no one found to return and give praise to God except this foreigner?"

It is interesting in verses twenty-five through twenty-eight that the Lord uses fierce lions attacking the people there in Israel to motivate the king of Assyria to send one of the priests of Israel back to his land to teach these transplanted Assyrians the worship of Jehovah.

The practice of transporting the citizens of one country to another was the custom of the Assyrians. This was their method of keeping down any rebellion that might occur after the invaders left.

Once the Assyrians took over the ten tribes of Israel, they decided eight years later to go after the other two tribes of Judah. The Assyrian king, Sennacherib, attacked all of Judah's fortified cities and captured them.

All except Jerusalem.

The King Sennacherib then sends his supreme commander, his chief officer, and his field commander with a large army to capture Jerusalem.

Hezekiah was the king of Judah at this time and the Scripture says of him in II Kings 18:5-7:

> *"Hezekiah trusted in the Lord, the God of Israel. There was no one like him among all the kings of Judah, either before him or after him. He held fast to the Lord and did not cease to follow him; he kept the commands the Lord had given Moses. And the Lord was with him; he was successful in whatever he undertook. He rebelled against the king of Assyria and did not serve him."*

Though Hezekiah rebelled against Assyria, he then submits and pays tribute money, but apparently that was not enough to turn back the Assyrian army from Jerusalem's gates.

The events of these activities are recorded in three main places in the Bible: II Kings 18 and 19; (18:13 - 19:37) II Chronicles 32; (1-22) and Isaiah 36 and 37.

What now follows is a summary of the miraculous deliverance of Jerusalem and the catastrophic defeat of the Assyrian army of 185,000 troops by one angel of God!

King Hezekiah prepares to defend Jerusalem and he assures the Judahites of God's help.

> *"After all that Hezekiah had so faithfully done, Sennacherib king of*

Assyria came and invaded Judah. He laid siege to the fortified cities, thinking to conquer them for himself. When Hezekiah saw that Sennacherib had come and that he intended to make war on Jerusalem, he consulted with his officials and military staff about blocking off the water from the springs outside the city, and they helped him. A large force of men assembled, and they blocked all the springs and the stream that flowed through the land. 'Why should the kings of Assyria come and find plenty of water?' they said. Then he worked hard repairing all the broken sections of the wall and building towers on it. He built another wall outside that one and reinforced the supporting terraces of the City of David. He also made large numbers of weapons and shields."

"He appointed military officers over the people and assembled them before him in the square at the city gate and encouraged them with these words: 'Be strong and courageous. Do not be afraid or discouraged because of the king of Assyria and the vast army with him, for there is a greater power with us than with him. With him is only the arm of flesh, but with us is the LORD our God to help us and to fight our battles.' And the people gained confidence from what Hezekiah the king of Judah said" (II Chronicles 32:1-8, NIV).

<u>The Assyrian king</u> sends his leaders to intimidate and terrify the Jews into surrendering their city of Jerusalem.

"The king of Assyria sent his supreme commander, his chief officer, and his field commander with a large army, from Lachish to King Hezekiah at Jerusalem. They came up to Jerusalem and stopped at the aqueduct of the Upper Pool, on the road to the Washerman's Field. They called for the king; and Eliakim son of Hilkiah the palace administrator, Shebna the secretary, and Joah son of Asaph the recorder went out to them.

The field commander said to them, "Tell Hezekiah: 'This is what the great king, the king of Assyria, says: On what are you basing this confidence of yours? You say you have strategy and military strength - but you speak only empty words. On whom are you depending, that you rebel against me? Look now, you are depending on Egypt, that splintered reed of a staff, which pierces a man's hand and wounds him if he leans on it! Such is Pharaoh king of Egypt to all who depend on him. And if you say to me, 'We are depending on the Lord our God' - isn't he the one whose high places and altars Hezekiah removed, saying to Judah and Jerusalem, 'You must worship before this altar in Jerusalem'?

"Come now, make a bargain with my master, the king of Assyria: I will give you two thousand horses, if you can put riders

on them. How can you repulse one officer of the last of my master's officials, even though you are depending on Egypt for chariots and horsemen? Furthermore, have I come to attack and destroy this place without word from the LORD? The Lord himself told me to march against this country and destroy it" (II Kings 18:17-25).

"Later, when Sennacherib king of Assyria and all his forces were laying siege to Lachish, he sent his officers to Jerusalem with this message for Hezekiah king of Judah and for all the people of Judah who were there:
"This is what Sennacherib king of Assyria says: On what are you basing your confidence, that you remain in Jerusalem under siege? When Hezekiah says, 'The Lord our God will save us from the hand of the king of Assyria,' he is misleading you, to let you die of hunger and thirst. Did not Hezekiah himself remove this god's high places and altars, saying to Judah and Jerusalem, 'You must worship before one altar and burn sacrifices on it'?
"Do you not know what I and my fathers have done to all the peoples of the other lands? Were the gods of those nations ever able to deliver their land from my hand? Who of all the gods of these nations that my fathers destroyed has been able to save his people from me? How then can your god deliver you from my hand. Now do not let Hezekiah deceive you and

mislead you like this. Do not believe him, for no god of any nation or kingdom has been able to deliver his people from my hand or the hand of my fathers. How much less will your god deliver you from my hand!"

"Sennacherib's officers spoke further against the LORD God and against his servant Hezekiah.

"The king also wrote letters insulting the LORD, the God of Israel, and saying this against him: 'Just as the gods of the peoples of the other lands did not rescue their people from my hand, so the god of Hezekiah will not rescue his people from my hand.' Then they called out in Hebrew to the people of Jerusalem who were on the wall, to terrify them and make them afraid in order to capture the city. They spoke about the God of Jerusalem as they did about the gods of the other peoples of the world - the work of men's hands" (II Chronicles 32:9-19).

"When the field commander heard that the king of Assyria had left Lachish, he withdrew and found the king fighting against Libnah.

"Now Sennacherib received a report that Tirhakah, the Cushite king of Egypt, was marching out to fight against him. When he heard it, he sent messengers to Hezekiah with this word: 'Say to Hezekiah king of Judah: Do not let the god you depend on deceive you when he says,

Jerusalem will not be handed over to the king of Assyria.' Surely you have heard what the kings of Assyria have done to all the countries, destroying them completely. And will you be delivered? Did the gods of the nations that were destroyed by my forefathers deliver them - the gods of Gozan, Haran, Rezeph and the people of Eden who were in Tel Assar? Where is the king of Hamath, the king of Arpad; the king of the city of Sepharvaim, or of Hena or Ivvah?" (Isaiah 37:8-13).

"The field commander said to them, 'Tell Hezekiah, This is what the great king, the king of Assyria, says: On what are you basing this confidence of yours? You say you have strategy and military strength - but you speak only empty words. On whom are you depending, that you rebel against me? Look now, you are depending on Egypt, that splintered reed of a staff, which pierces a man's hand and wounds him if he leans on it! Such is Pharaoh king of Egypt to all who depend on him. And if you say to me, 'We are depending on the LORD our God' - isn't he the one whose high places and altars Hezekiah removed, saying to Judah and Jerusalem, 'You must worship before this altar'?

"Come now, make a bargain with my master, the king of Assyria: I will give you two thousand horses, if you can put riders on them. How then can you repulse one officer of the least of my master's officials, even though you are depending on Egypt for chariots and horsemen? Furthermore, have I come to attack and destroy this land without the LORD? The LORD himself told me to march against this country and destroy it'" (Isaiah 36:4-10).

Speak in Aramaic (Assyrian) language.
"Then Eliakim son of Kilkiah, and shebna and Joah said to the field commander, 'Please speak to your servants in Aramaic, since we understand it. Don't speak to us in Hebrew in the hearing of the people on the wall'." (II Kings 18:26).
Insults!
"But the commander replied, 'Was it only to your master and you that my master sent me to say these things, and not to the men sitting on the wall - who like you, will have to eat their own filth and drink their own urine?'

"Then the commander stood and called out in Hebrew: 'Hear the word of the great king, the king of Assyria! This is what the king says: Do not let Hezekiah deceive you. He cannot deliver you from my hand. Do not let Hezekiah persuade you to trust in the LORD when he says, 'The LORD will surely deliver us; this city will not be given into the hand of the king of Assyria'.

"Do not listen to Hezekiah. This is what the king of Assyria says: Make peace with me and come out to me. Then every one of you will eat from his own vine and fig tree and drink water from his own cistern, until I come and take you to a land like your own, a land of grain and new wine, a land of bread and vineyards, a land of olive trees and honey. Choose life and not death!

"Do not listen to Hezekiah, for he is misleading you when he says, `The LORD will deliver us.' Has the god of any nation ever delivered his land from the hand of the king of Assyria? Where are the gods of Hamath and Arpad? Where are the gods of Sepharvaim, Hena and Ivvah? Have they rescued Samaria from my hand? Who of all the gods of these countries has been able to save his land from me? How then can the LORD deliver Jerusalem from my hand?

"But the people remained silent and said nothing in reply, because the king had commanded, `Do not answer him.'

"Then Eliakim son of Hilkiah the palace administrator, Shebna the secretary and Joah son of Asaph the recorder went to Hezekiah, with their clothes torn, and told him what the field commander had said" (II Kings 18:27-37).

King Hezekiah turns to God in prayer.

"When King Hezekiah heard this, he tore his clothes and put on sackcloth and went into the temple of the LORD. He sent Eliakim the palace administrator, shebna the secretary and the leading priests, all wearing sackcloth, to the prophet Isaiah son of Amoz. They told him, `This is what

Hezekiah says: This day is a day of distress and rebuke and disgrace, as when children come to the point of birth and there is no strength to deliver them. It may be that the LORD your God will hear all the words of the field commander, whom his master, the king of Assyria, has sent to ridicule the living God, and that he will rebuke him for the words the LORD your God has heard. Therefore pray for the remnant that still survives" (II Kings 19:1-4).

"Hezekiah received the letter from the messengers and read it. Then he went up to the temple of the LORD and spread it out before the LORD. And Hezekiah prayed to the LORD: 'O LORD, God of Israel, enthroned between the cherubim, you alone are God over all the kingdoms of the earth. You have made heaven and earth. Give ear, O Lord, and hear; open your eyes, O LORD, and see; listen to the words Sennacherib has sent to insult the living God.

"It is true, O LORD, that the Assyrian kings have laid waste these nations and their lands. They have thrown their gods into the fire and destroyed them, for they were not gods but only wood and stone, fashioned by men's hands. Now, O LORD our God, deliver us from his hand, so that all kingdoms on earth may know that you alone, O LORD, are God" (II Kings 19: 14-19).

"King Hezekiah and the prophet Isaiah son of Amoz cried out in prayer to heaven about this" (II Chronicles 32:20).

"When King Hezekiah heard this, he tore his clothes and put on sackcloth and went into the temple of the LORD. He sent Eliakim the palace administrator, Shebna the secretary, and the leading priests, all wearing sackcloth, to the prophet Isaiah son of Amoz. They told him, 'This is what Hezekiah says: This day is a day of distress and rebuke and disgrace, as when children come to the point of birth and there is no strength to deliver them. It may be that the LORD your God will hear the words of the field commander, whom his master, the king of Assyria, has sent to ridicule the living God, and that he will rebuke him for the words the LORD your God has heard. Therefore pray for the remnant that still survives'" (Isaiah 37:1-4).

"Hezekiah received the letter from the messengers and read it. Then he went up to the temple of the LORD and spread it out before the LORD. And Hezekiah prayed to the LORD: 'O LORD Almighty, God of Israel, enthroned between the cherubim, you alone are God over all the kingdoms of the earth. You have made heaven and earth. Give ear, O LORD, and hear; open your eyes, O LORD, and see; listen to all the words Sennacherib has sent to insult the living God.

"Is it true, O LORD, that the Assyrian kings have laid waste all these peoples and *their lands. They have thrown their gods into the fire and destroyed them, for they were not gods but only wood and stone, fashioned by human hands. Now, O LORD our God, deliver us from his hand, so that all kingdoms on earth may know that you alone, O LORD, are God" (Isaiah 37:14-20).*

The prophet Isaiah prophecies defeat of Assyrians.

"When King Hezekiah's officials came to Isaiah, Isaiah said to them, 'Tell your master, This is what the LORD says: Do not be afraid of what you have heard - those words with which the underlings of the king of Assyria have blasphemed me. Listen! I am going to put such a spirit in him that when he hears a certain report, he will return to his own country, and there I will have him cut down with the sword'" (II Kings 19: 5-7).

"Then Isaiah son of Amoz sent a message to Hezekiah: 'This is what the LORD, the God of Israel, says: I have heard your prayer concerning Sennacherib king of Assyria. This is the word that the LORD has spoken against him:

The Virgin Daughter of Zion
despises you and mocks you.
The Daughter of Jerusalem
tosses her head as you flee.
Who is it you have insulted and blasphemed?
Against whom have you raised you voice
and lifted your eyes in pride?

Against the Holy One of Israel!
By your messengers
you have heaped insults on the Lord.
And you have said,
'With my many chariots
I have ascended the heights of the mountains,
the utmost heights of Lebanon.
I have cut down its tallest cedars,
the choicest of its pines.
I have reached its remotest parts,
the finest of its forests.
I have dug wells in foreign lands
and drunk the water there.
With the soles of my feet
I have dried up all the streams of Egypt.'
Have you not heard?
Long ago I ordained it.
In days of old I planned it;
now I have brought it to pass,
that you have turned fortified cities
into piles of stone.
Their people, drained of power,
are dismayed and put to shame.
They are like plants in the field,
like tender green shoots,
like grass sprouting on the housetops,
scorched before it grows up.
But I know where you stay
and when you come and go
and how you rage against me.
Because you rage against me
and your insolence has reached my ears,

I will put my hook in your nose
and my bit in your mouth,
and I will make you return
by the way you came.'
This will be the sign for you, O
Hezekiah:
This year you will eat what grows by
itself,
and the second year what springs from
that.
But in the third year sow and reap,
plant vineyards and eat their fruit.
Once more a remnant of the house of
Judah
will take root below and bear fruit
above.
For out of Jerusalem will come a
remnant,
and out of Mount Zion a band of
survivors.
The zeal of the LORD Almighty will
accomplish this.
Therefore this is what the LORD says
concerning the king of Assyria:
He will not enter this city
or shoot an arrow here.
He will not come before it with shield
or build a siege ramp against it.
By the way that he came he will return;
he will not enter this city,
declares the LORD,
I will defend this city and save it,
for my sake and for the sake of David
my servant" (II Kings 10:20-34).
<u>The miraculous defeat of the Assyrian army</u>.

"That night the angel of the LORD went out and put to death a hundred and eighty-five thousand men in the Assyrian camp. When the people got up the next morning - there were all the dead bodies! So Sennacherib king of Assyria broke camp, and withdrew. He returned to Nineveh and stayed there.

"One day, while he was worshiping in the temple of his god Nisroch, his sons Adrammelech and Sharezer cut him down with the sword, and they escaped to the land of Ararat. And Esarhaddon his son succeeded him as king" (II Kings 19:35-37).

"And the LORD sent an angel, who annihilated all the fighting men and the leaders and officers in the camp of the Assyrian king. So he withdrew to his own land in disgrace. And when he went into the temple of his god, some of his sons cut him down with the sword" (II Chronicles 32:21).

This is one of the greatest, supernatural battles in the Bible!

Think of it - 185,000 crack troops conquered Egypt, all of that land, the ten tribes, and then come against Jerusalem.

This is one of the greatest supernatural battles in the Bible.

Hezekiah prays; he calls on God.

God sends one angel.

Just one angel saved Jerusalem!

God sends one angel.

Just one angel saved Jerusalem!

And that single angel wiped out 185,000 Assyrians! In one stroke.

Talk about a weapon more powerful than a scud missile!

Could this happen again today?

Of course it could. God has not changed.

IF ONLY A NATION WILL CALL UPON GOD, HE WILL SPARE THEM!

"If my people, which are called by my name, shall humble themselves, and pray, and seek my face, and turn from their wicked ways; then will I hear from heaven, and will forgive their sin, and will heal their land" (II Chronicles 7:14).

Assyria as a nation started having a downfall - the official date for the fall of the Assyrian Empire is 612 B.C. They were conquered by combined forces of the Medes, Scythians, and Babylonians. The Assyrians started to dwindle and lost power; Assyria became Mesopotamia.

The official date for the fall of Jerusalem is July 18, 586 B.C. From that time forward, the Jews were a scattered nation until May, 1948.

Throughout history, only two nations have been without a country for thousands of years, and yet have been able to maintain their identity... **the Israelites and the Assyrians!**

In 1948, the Israelites regained their country.

As you shall see soon in this book, God also has an entire plan for the Assyrians.

The Assyrians were unable to recover the might and power they once built and maintained for more than two millennia. Thereafter, they fell victim to many atrocities that reduced their numbers to a small nation living at the mercy of their overlords in the vastly scattered lands of the Middle Eastern region.

And today, the territory that was once called Assyria is called Iraq.

Iraq is basically where <u>Mesopotamia</u> was, and Mesopotamia is where Assyria was. In this endtime generation of spiritual history, I believe that we are soon going to see God unleash something remarkable in this region.

CHAPTER FIVE

GOD'S OTHER "FAVORED NATION" - THE ASSYRIANS!

The whole book of Jonah is about Assyria, and God wanting to spare Nineveh, which He did. God said to Jonah,

> "Arise, go to Nineveh, that great city, and cry against it; for their wickedness is come up before me" (Jonah 1:2).

From a human standpoint, Assyria was the last place Jonah as an Israelite prophet would choose for a mission. He had to tell approximately one million Ninevites that in 40 days their city would be destroyed (Jonah 3:4).

Well, Jonah did finally go, and warned the Assyrians, and they heeded his warnings and repented. The repentance under Jonah delayed the judgment of God on Assyria for about a century. (The entire book of Nahum concerns Assyria, and forms the sequel to the Book of Jonah).

> "So the people of Nineveh believed God, and proclaimed a fast, and put on sackcloth, from the greatest of them even to the least of them.
> For word came unto the king of Nineveh, and he arose from his throne, and

he laid his robe before him, and covered him with sackcloth, and sat in ashes.

"And he caused it to be proclaimed and published through Nineveh by the decree of the king and his nobles, saying, Let neither man nor beast, herd nor flock, taste any thing: let them not feed, nor drink water:

"But let man and beast be covered with sackcloth, and cry mightily unto God: yea, let them turn every one from his evil way, and from the violence that is in their hands.

"Who can tell if God will turn and repent, and turn away from his fierce anger, that we perish not?" (Jonah 3:5-9).

By their repenting, God spared Nineveh.

"And God saw their works that they turned from their evil way and God repented of the evil that he had said that he would do unto them; and he did not" (Jonah 3:10).

In repentance, God spared the Assyrians.

Now that is something significant!

Scripture shows here that the first confrontation the Assyrians had with God was about 782-753 B.C., revealed in the accounting of the Book of Jonah.

The Assyrian king at that time was either Adad-Nirari III (810-782 B.C) or Ashur-Dan III (782-753 B.C.).

This is during the height of the Assyrian empire.

As we read the four chapters of Book of Jonah in God's Holy Word, we can learn what may be called "the five greats": the great refusal, the great fish, the great city, the great jealousy, and the great God.

In the first chapter, God commands Jonah to "Arise, go to Nineveh, that great city".

Here we see that God regarded the Assyrian city as great. In Jonah 3:3, it is described as "an exceedingly great city".

As we saw earlier in this book, the history of the Assyrian people clearly reveals the many great contributions they made to the world.

When Jonah is first instructed to go to the Assyrians, he foolishly tries to flee from God, and in his flight (aboard a ship) the Lord creates a tempest and Jonah is thrown overboard.

The second chapter is Jonah's prayer of thanksgiving to the Lord for delivering him from the Great Fish:

"Now the LORD had prepared a great fish to swallow up Jonah. And Jonah was in the belly of the fish three days and three nights" (Jonah 1:17).

In chapter three, God again calls Jonah to go to Nineveh (the great city).

This time he <u>does respond</u> and goes.

God instructs Jonah to cry out and say, "Yet forty days and Nineveh shall be overthrown" (Jonah 3:4).

From these prophetic warnings, the Assyrians proclaimed a fast and put on sackcloth. Even the king and his nobles repented and put on sackcloth and sat in ashes.

When God saw how they turned from their evil ways, He forgave them.

This is the first confrontation God has with the Assyrians, and because of their faith, God blesses them, and they became a favored nation.

In the fourth chapter, we find Jonah pouting. He becomes jealous because God blesses the Assyrians and makes them mighty warriors (the great jealousy). The entire book of Jonah is a powerful lesson in the power of pray, and in the power of repentance.

Someday, the leaders of the world are going to come to the Christians - to discover the real wisdom of God's Word and the real power in the universe.

To know God's Word is to know His will. To know His will is to know His Word.
The wisdom of God is what the world will eventually seek.

Oh how great is the grace of God to the Assyrians and to all people who will turn from their sins and sinful ways to the Lord Jesus Christ and in faith receive Him into their lives and live in a relationship based upon obedience to God's Word as revealed in the Bible by the Holy Spirit!

Jesus Christ regarded this account of Jonah and the Assyrians as an historical fact. In the Gospel of Luke, chapter 11 and verses 30 and 32, He said:

"As Jonah was a sign to the Ninevites, so shall also the Son of Man be to this generation. The men of Nineveh shall rise up in judgment with this generation, and shall condemn it; for they reprented at the preaching of Jonah; and behold, a greter than Jonah is here."

Jesus referred to Jonah as a sign of His own resurrection. He put the great fish, the repentance of the Assyrians in Nineveh, his resurrection, and the judgment day in the same category when he spoke in the Gospel of Matthew about *"the sign of the prophet Jonah."* In Chapter 12 and verse 40, Jesus said:

> *"For as Jonah was three days and three nights in the belly of the huge fish; so shall the Son of Man be three days and three nights in the heart of the earth."*

When Jesus was on earth, the Assyrians were co-mingled with the ten tribes of Israel, so they heard Jesus (when Jesus told the apostles not to go to the Gentiles or the Samaritans, but to the lost sheep of the house of Israel - He meant these ten tribes)...the lost sheep of the house of Israel.

The Assyrians were there as well as the Jews. The Assyrians were exposed to Christianity at the time of Jesus, and church history tells us that the apostles sent Thadeous to King Abgar of Osrhoene to bring the Assyrians the gospel.

This is something few Christians know:
THE ASSYRIANS WERE THE FIRST GENTILE NATION TO TURN TO JESUS CHRIST!

On the day of Pentecost, they were there as Mesopotamians. They were from all over.

> *"And there were dwelling at Jerusalem Jews, devout men, out of every nation under heaven" (Acts 2:5).*
> *"Parthians, and Medes, and Elamites, and the dwellers in Mesopotamia, and in*

Judea, and Cappadocia, in Pontus, and Asia," (Acts 2:9).

They were baptized in the Holy Spirit and went back to Mesopotamia with the Baptism in the Holy Spirit.

And the ancient church of the east became one of the greatest missionary churches of all time!

The Assyrians ventured as far as India, Japan and China with the gospel.

They were among the first people to embrace Christianity as a nation in the first century, and they played a great role in taking Christianity to the vast continent of Asia, converting their civilized and uncivilized peoples. They journeyed to the shores of the Mediterranean Sea and into the Mongolian deserts and even into China and Japan.

The first Christian nation was Assyria!

So what has happened?

God is going to use these same Christians in this endtime hour in the fulfillment of the prophecy in Isaiah 19: 23-25:

> *"In that day there will be a highway from Egypt to Assyria. The Assyrians will go to Egypt and the Egyptians to Assyria. The Egyptians and Assyrians will worship together.*
>
> *"In that day Israel will be the third, along with Egypt and Assyria, a blessing on the earth.*
>
> *"The Lord Almighty will bless them, saying, 'Blessed be Egypt my people,*

Assyria my handiwork, and Israel my inheritance'" (Isaiah 19:23-25, NIV).

"In that day" there will be a highway from Egypt to Assyria. The highway is named in Isaiah 35:8 - it is called "The Highway of Holiness."

"In that day" always refers to the endtime hour of spiritual history.

The Assyrians will go to Egypt and the Egyptians throughout Assyria.

I believe God can accomplish His endtime task in the same way, fulfilling Isaiah 19.

Isaiah 19 is the most thrilling passage of Scripture, and many prophets and Bible teachers continually refer to it.

I have written that Assyria is a forgotten nation, but it is not forgotten by God.

Assyria is a lost country, but not by God.

I want to tell you this.

God in His mercy is so good to Assyria.

The Egyptians and Assyrians will worship together <u>in that day</u>, and Israel will be one of three nations (along with Egypt and Assyria) - <u>to be a blessing on the earth</u>.

These three nations, God says, will be a blessing on the earth. The Lord Almighty will bless them saying, "Blessed be Egypt my people."

"Blessed be Assyria, the work of my hands."

You know what it means to be God's handiwork?

Assyria will be a work done by God's hands.

Just as God had an endtime plan for the Israelites, He has an endtime plan for the Assyrians!

This prophetic Scripture indicates that in the last days the Egyptians will befriend the Assyrians and they will both befriend the nation of Israel.

God intends to use Assyria again in this endtime hour!

Look at Micah 7:11-12:

> *"In the day that thy walls are to be built, in that day shall the decree be far removed.*
> *"In that day also he shall come even to thee from Assyria, and from the fortified cities, and from the fortress even to the river, and from the sea to sea, and from mountain to mountain."*

That means Assyria must exist in the endtime hour!

The people who were converted at the time of Christ and the apostles, and have maintained their faithfulness to God for over 2,000 years, will have their nation restored once again, just as the Jews had their nation restored!

Yet, from the first confrontation (Jonah) through the ages, we see a definite link between God and the Assyrians.

They are his holy instrument.

I have not heard the details of this prophecy discussed anywhere except when I bring up the subject.

Others are not talking about it or writing about it. If it is of God, I pray you may be able to take it.

If it is not, well, then it is my idea.

But the Word seems clear in what it says here to me.

The nations - Egypt, Assyria and Israel - are to be nations blessed in the endtime.

Symbolically, I believe they represent the three religions in the Middle East.

What religions do we have there?

We have Islam - the religion of the Egyptians.

We have Christianity - the religion of the Assyrians.

We have the Jewish faith - the religion of the Israelites.

According to Isaiah 19, blessed be Egypt my people. The Egyptians are Islamic. The Egyptians and Islam will bow to Jesus Christ.

Assyria is the Christian nation.

Israel represents the Jews.

Think about it.

The Jews, Christians and Islamics together will be blessed of God because they will all be worshipping Jehovah God, receiving Jesus Christ as Savior!

Now that is exciting!

The Assyrians as a united people already are all professing to be Christians.

However, they need to have a revival because they are saying they are the ancient church of the east, they speak the Assyrian language, Aramaic. Their Masses are in Aramaic.

There is still the need for many of these beloved people to be "born-again."

Yes, they believe devoutly in Jesus Christ.

But they have to have a real born-again experience, which I believe will soon take place.

In this endtime, we will see a sovereign, almighty, powerful work of God.

JONAH AND THE WORM

When Jonah came out of the belly of the whale,
He went straight to Nineveh and did them assail;
With powerful preaching and pending destruction,
So that the entire city was in disruption.

Then upon man and beast the King proclaimed a fast,
Hoping that God's anger upon them would not last.
When God saw their repentance then He had pity,
And said He would not destroy that wicked city.

When Jonah left there he went east and there sat down,
Waiting for the Lord to destroy that wicked town.
After forty days had passed and nothing occurred,
Then Jonah was angry and greatly disturbed.

So then for Jonah God prepared a great big gourd,
And in the shade of it he sat and slep and snoed.
A big worm that God prepared then came crawling by,
Ate a big hole in the gourd and caused it to die.

Then Jonah was angry with God and wanted to die,
And said, "I have a right to be angry; haven't I?"
Then God said, "For that gourd that died you had pity,
And you're angry because I pitied a city."

T'was a worm God used to teach Jonah a lesson,
T'was only a worm but Jonah lost the blessin'.
T'was a worm that God used brother Jonah to try,
But Jonah was so made that he wanted to die.

How many Jonahs there are in the land today,
Who go on a big pout when things don't go their way.
Some get real angry like brother Jonah of old,
And justify themselves when of their fault they're told.

When they get real angry they never feel condemned.
They never repent and their ways they never mend.
Like brother Jonah of old they feel justified,
And so in their bad temper they often take pride.

It took a trip in a whole to stop Jonah's flight,
And it took a gourd and a wom to set Jonah right.
So I wonder wht the good Lord will have to do,
With some folks who get angry every day or two.

Rev. Charles Vander Ploeg

82

CHAPTER SIX

A SMALL SIGN OF THE PROPHECY COMES TO PASS!

I am Assyrian.

I was invited, along with our Congressman, Mark Siljander, to go to Israel in 1983 at the invitation of the government's Herut Party. They paid my way, and our Congressman was the door opener for me.

In Jerusalem, on May 31, 1983, I had the opportunity to meet with the Prime Minister of Israel, Menachem Begin.

As we met, I said to him, "I am here in your country of Israel as a representative of Intercessors for America. We pray for America, but we also remember to pray for Israel each day."

Prime Minister Menachem Begin (left) greets Rev. John Booko in Jerusalem in 1983.

Prime Minister Begin was obviously pleased by this information, and he replied, "I want to thank all the Christians who support us."

"We certainly do," I responded.

Two years later, **in 1985**, the Egyptian foundation invited me to visit their country along with our Congressman who was on the Middle East sub-committee.   On that visit, **I was given the opportunity to visit Egyptian President Hosni Mubarak in his Presidential Palace** in Cairo.

Our American ambassador   was there; the foreign minister was there; so were a number of dignitaries.

(See photo of this historic meeting on page 88 of this book).

I silently prayed, "Lord, give me an opening here with Mubarak, the Egyptian president."

God did.

After our official meeting, when I was shaking hands with the Egyptian president, God gave me a holy boldness. I said, "Mr. President, I represent Intercessors for America. We pray for God to bless America. May I have the honor of praying for you and your nation?"

To my surprise, he said, "Yes."

So I had the opportunity to pray in his presence and asked God to bless him and his nation.

I prayed,

> *Dear Heavenly Father,*
> *We thank you for your love and power.*
> *I ask your blessing on President Mubarak and the people of this country.*

I pray for your wisdom and strength upon President Mubarak. I thank you that he is a man of peace. Your Word has said "Blessed are the peacemakers, for they shall be called the children of God".

Thank you for your blessing upon this nation and president. Amen.

When I finished praying, he thanked me and gave me a warm hug.

I cannot help but believe in my mind that these small but symbolic meetings were a forerunner of Isaiah 19: 23-25.

"In that day there will be a highway from Egypt to Assyria. The Assyrians will go to Egypt and the Egyptians to Assyria. The Egyptians and Assyrians will worship together.

"In that day Israel will be the third, along with Egypt and Assyria, a blessing on the earth.

"The Lord Almighty will bless them, saying, 'Blessed be Egypt my people, Assyria my handiwork, and Israel my inheritance'" (Isaiah 19:23-25, NIV).

Scriptures proclaim that the Egyptians and the Assyrians will worship together!

You may wonder, "Why didn't you personally ask to pray with Menachem Begin?"

To be honest, I did not have a leading at the time (not realizing that this was falling right into the prophecy of Isaiah 19).

It was only later I realized that I perhaps became a little sign (and I give God all the glory and credit for this) of the fulfillment of Isaiah 19:23-25.

Why?

Because I am the Assyrian.

I met with both the Israeli Prime Minister, Menachem Begin, and then with the Egyptian President, Hosni Mubarak.

Now think of the odds of that!.

Of course, many people visit the Prime Minister of Israel - but where are you going to get an Assyrian?

Well, God picked one out of a little town called "Three Rivers, Michigan", with a population of about 7,500.

God used a little Assyrian preacher filled with the Holy Spirit, putting him in meetings with officials from BOTH Israel and Egypt!

Nothing is too difficult for God.

When the Lord declares His word, then one angel can defeat 185,000 troops, and one unknown Assyrian can meet with the heads of Israel and Egypt.

The Apostle Paul said God spoke to him in Aramaic on the road to Damascus. The voice that came out of Heaven was Aramaic (Acts 26:14, NIV).

But I want to give you the last word in Aramaic that did not get translated - but just transliterated. It is 1 Corinthians 16:22 and the word is Maran-atha.

>*"If any man love not the Lord Jesus*
>*Christ, let him be Anathema, Maranatha"*
>*(I Corinthians 16:22).*

The Assyrian, Aramaic rendering is "Maran," meaning "Our Lord", and "atah," which means "to come."

Hence, the last Assyrian word in the Bible means our Lord comes.

And when He comes, then Isaiah 19 will be fulfilled!

Maranatha.

The Lord comes!

All these things will be fulfilled in exact accordance with the scriptures.

But the prophet also declares that Israel will be living at peace with her neighbors.

Egypt must keep a peace treaty.

Jordan, right now a key enemy of Israel, will have to make a peace treaty.

Syria, another neighbor, and Lebanon, both will need to make peace treaties.

Conceivably, there will be yet another small war between Israel and Syria, and possibly Iraq will enter into this situation to dismember Syria - because that ultimately will be necessary for an alignment of peace.

If we look at Isaiah 19, we find that there is going to be a spiritual revival encompassing Egypt, Israel and Assyria.

And since Assyria does not now exist, but modern day Iraq and Northern Syria comprise what used to be called Assyria, I would see the beginning of the ascendancy of Iraq in the Middle East to be extremely significant because ultimately Iraq will turn against Syria or Syria will turn against Iraq and be beaten by Iraq and Israel, following which there will be peace between these former enemies and **the NEW ASSYRIA**.

It will happen according to the Bible!

And so, the immediate neighbors, possibly even Saudi Arabia, will ultimately be at peace with Israel, and then some members of the Commonwealth of Independent States, in the new Soviet confederation, will begin to move against Israel.

God gave me the opportunity to pray with Egyptian President Hosni Mubarak, in Cairo, Egypt, on April 7, 1985 (accompanied by Congressman Mark Siljander).

CHAPTER SEVEN

RUSSIA WILL INVADE ISRAEL!
(NOT the Battle of Armageddon)

In these next few chapters, I am going to attempt to help you understand some of the basic events you will see take place in biblical prophecy before the ascendency of Assyria as a nation will be fulfilled.

One of the first is the invasion of Israel by Russia (now called the Commonwealth of Independent States).

Until just recently - the thought of Russia (CIS) invading Israel seemed impossible.

Russia (CIS), led by President Gorbachev, was a nation proclaiming "peace" to the world through arms reduction treaties. Gorbachev was increasing his pledges to cooperate with other nations to bring Capitalism and Democracy to the Soviet Union.

But, on August 19, 1991, a coup was launched, and an attempt to overthrow Gorbachev took place!

A new RUSSIAN GOVERNMENT was installed!

VIRTUALLY OVERNIGHT, the political face of Russia (CIS) changed.

Although this coup was ultimately defeated, it clearly shows that Russia (CIS) is not the stable, peace-loving, democratic society many believe it is becoming. Gorbachev ultimately resigned as President of the former Soviet Union, and Boris

Yeltsin is now leading "The Commonwealth of Independent states of Russia."

Expect this new nation to continue to use their military strength to achieve their objectives - against any nation, any time, and especially, against Israel.

Now that they are breaking Russia (CIS) up into independent states, there are several Russian states which are heavily Muslim, and are bitter enemies of Israel (at least five).

Any one of them could be the catalyst in launching an offensive against Israel.

Ezekiel 38 and 39 give a detailed account of a great military offensive launched against Israel by Russia (CIS) and a confederation of Arab and European counties.

In modern terms, the countries involved will probably be Russia (CIS), Germany, Turkey, Iran, Ethiopia and Libya.

Russia (CIS) will lead the invasion.

Daniel tells us:

> *"And at the time of the end shall the king of the south (Arab and African confederacy) push at him: and the king of the north (Russia (CIS) and confederates) shall come against him like a whirlwind, with chariots, and with horsemen, and with many ships; and he shall enter into the countries, and shall overflow and pass over" (Daniel 11:40).*

Russia (CIS) will attack Israel "to take a spoil."

The most likely reason for the attack would be to control the flow of oil through the Middle East.

"Go up to the land of unwalled villages; I will go to them that are at rest, and dwell safely, all of them dwelling without walls, and having neither bars nor gates, to take a spoil, and to take a prey... upon the people that are gathered out of the nations..." (Ezekiel 38: 11-12).

Russia's attack will prove to be a major military blunder.

The defeat of Russia (CIS) will make it clear to the Jews that God has protected them.

God is going to supernaturally intervene and the war will be won through the signs and wonders He manifests on Israel's behalf (remember, one angel against 185,000 troops?).

"But in that day when Gog (Russia - CIS) shall come against the land of Israel, says the Lord God, My wrath shall come up into My nostrils. For in My jealousy and in the fire of My wrath have I said, Surely in that day there shall be a great shaking (cosmic catastrophe) in the land of Israel; So that the fishes of the sea, and the birds of the heavens, and the beasts of the field, and all creeping things that creep upon the earth, and all the men that are upon the face of the earth, shall tremble and shake at My presence, and the mountains shall be thrown down, and the steep places shall fall, and every wall

(natural or artificial) shall fall to the ground" (Ezekiel 38:18-20, TLB)

Ezekiel says only **one-sixth** of Russia's great army will escape death in the battle.

"And I will turn thee back, and leave but the sixth part of thee" (Ezekiel 39:2).

So many will die that it will take Israel seven months to bury all the bodies left behind, and the burning of the weapons will go on for seven years.

"And they that dwell in the cities of Israel shall go forth, and shall set on fire and burn the weapons, both the shields and the bucklers, the bows and the arrows, and the handstaves, and the spears, and they shall burn them with fire seven years:" (Ezekiel 39:9).

Someone may ask, "Brother John, how is it possible for weapons to burn for seven years?"

Two ways:

One - The atomic charge in some of the Russian weapons could be converted to a long-lasting fuel supply.

Two - Many Russian weapons are made from lignostone, a special wood process resembling thirty or so pieces of plywood pressed together by dynamic steam pressure. Lignostone is stronger than steel, and very elastic; it burns better and longer than coal.

So, the actual weapons captured during the battle could be burned by Israel.

When the nation of Israel sees the signs and wonders God manifests on their behalf to miraculously deliver them out of the hands of their enemies during this war, <u>from that day forward</u> they will know and recognize beyond all question that He is the Lord their God.

After this war, expect to see a major shift in the balance of world power.

Since Russia (CIS) looses five-sixths of their invading army, they will cease to be a military threat in the world. This shift in military power will furnish the political and military climate for the rise of the Antichrist out of the European community (we will see in another chapter that the Antichrist is also called "the Assyrian").

Now, is Israel all that rich?

Well, the answer is "No, it isn't."

But there are riches in that area that are coveted by their enemies.

The oil in the Middle East is absolutely critical to world expansion and to Western economic growth. The oil from OPEC and the Arab nations fuels the industrial machine of Western Europe. Germany, Italy, France, the low countries are all dependent on OPEC oil.

If Russia (CIS) can claim control of that oil, she will have control of Europe. I believe that will be her motivation as she moves in God's plan as an endtime pawn to a pathetic and devastating defeat.

CHAPTER EIGHT

THE WANDERING ASSYRIANS

Today, the Kurds are in Northern Iraq.

100,000 Assyrians are in the same area.

In 1933, many Assyrians were massacred by the Iraqis.

Since World War II, their situation has changed for the worse in Iran - where they are suspected of collaborating with the Russians, and are now returning to Iraq.

For generations, the Assyrians had lived in the mountainous region in the vicinity of the Iranian, Iraqi, Syrian, and Turkish borders.

They are the descents from the ancient Assyrians. When Nineveh, the capital of the Assyrian Empire, fell in 612 B.C., many fled to the north, where their descendants continued to live for the next two-and-a-half millennia.

Much like the Jews, for decades they have wandered throughout the world without a country.

The latter-day Assyrians are a small, veteran Christian community who pray in the same Syrian-Aramaic dialect spoken by the inhabitants of Babylonia in ages past.

This small Christian sect is closed in on all sides by a sea of Muslims: Turks, Kurds, Persians, and Arabs - both Shiites and Sunnis - who are often in conflict among themselves but invariably are hostile to these unusual Christians.

Much like the Jews, the life of the Assyrians has therefore never been a blissful one: hardship, persecution, massacres and wars are their standard lot.

They are often called "The wandering Assyrians."

For weeks in 1991, the anguish of Kurdish refugees was front-page news.

Yet, among the Iraqi refugees is another, smaller ethnic group, one that has suffered Hussein's repression, but with much less attention from the press.

An estimated 500,000 Assyrian Christians, the descendants of a religious community at least 1,500 years old, have also fled their homes. According to the Middle East Council of Churches, most of these Assyrians are active in their Christian faith. Like the Kurds, the Aramaic-speaking group long for autonomous rule of their own territory. They have suffered death and illness brought on by dehydration, hunger, and cold.

The Assyrians of Iraq, of whom their American cousins number at about 300,000 are an oppressed minority - like the Kurds, only more so, because they are not even Muslims, so they are hated and despised for their religious beliefs.   The ancient Assyrians ruled the Beth-Nahrain, the land between the Tigris and Euphrates rivers, from about 1100 B.C. to 612 B.C., when their empire fell to civil war and foreign invasion.

Converted to Christianity in the first century A.D., they have been persecuted ever since. Among Kurdish rebels killed in Saddam Hussein's notorious chemical gas attacks during the Iran-Iraq War were several hundred Assyrian nationalists.

There were reports of mass graves of Assyrian babies. Forty Assyrian men reportedly returned to their villages in late April, 1991, only to be buried alive by remnants of Iraq's army.

Since 1988, over two hundred Assyrian villages have been destroyed by Hussein, says Albert Yelda, spokesman for the London-based Assyrian Cultural and Advice Center.

The Society for Threatened People, based in Germany, recently reported that over the past two decades, Hussein's regime killed 200,000 Kurds and 20,000 Assyrians. The numbers will jump much higher when the refugee death toll is finally added.

In many ways, the Assyrians are the American Indians of Iraq - they were there first, yet they now are disenfranchised.

Their hope is that America and others will help them create an autonomous Assyrian state - the first in 2,600 years. A Christian presence in that region would be a stabilizing influence.

They share a dream of independence, but fear a repeat of past betrayal, and cannot stomach war with a country in which friends and relatives still live.

<u>WITHOUT GOD, YOU CANNOT.</u>
<u>WITHOUT YOU, HE WILL NOT!</u>

The spiritual and the political arm must work together in unity!

<u>EUPHRATES RIVER TO BE DRIED UP</u>:

In Revelation 16:12 the Bible predicts that the Euphrates River will be dried up to prepare the way for the kings of the east to invade Israel. This will happen at the time of the battle of Armageddon according to verse 16 of the same chapter. The battle of Armageddon will be the final battle at which time Jesus Christ will return and fight on the side of the nation of Israel. Immediately thereafter He will establish His kingdom and usher in His 1000 year reign of peace.

On January 13th, 1990, the *Indianapolis Star* carried the headline "Turkey will cut off flow of Euphrates for 1 month." The article stated that a huge reservoir had been built by Turkey. While filling up the reservoir, the flow of the Euphrates would be stopped for one month and a concrete plug for a diversion channel built. These things have now been done. With this newly built dam, Turkey has the ability to stop the Euphrates River at will. The conditions for fulfilling this 1900 year old prophecy are now in place!

CHAPTER NINE

THE ANTICHRIST APPEARS -
SIGNING A SEVEN-YEAR COVENANT
WITH ISRAEL

Out of the ashes and over the dead bodies of millions of people slaughtered from the Russia (CIS)/Israel conflict will arise a ten-toed European kingdom which will have the strength of iron and the weakness of clay (Daniel 2:40-45). I will not detail that complete scenario of nations here, since that is not the purpose of this book.

This ten-divisioned kingdom will be formed in Europe, but within the boundaries of the old Roman Empire. The beginning of this union is observable in the highly successful European "Common Market," the goal of which is a political union and a universal currency for all of the European states.

At the head of this "United States of Europe" will rise a president - the Antichrist. It is during the beginning of his career as executive head of this European federation that he will make a seven-year covenant with Israel, which opens the way for Israel to construct a temple and begin sacrifices.

"And he shall confirm the covenant with many for one week (seven years): and in the midst of the week he shall cause the sacrifice and the oblation to cease, and for the overspreading of

abominations he shall make it desolate, even until the consummation, and that determined shall be poured upon the desolate" *(Daniel 9:27)*.

The Antichrist comes to power by deceit, promises of "peace," and threats of war and socialism.

"He shall enter peaceably even upon the fattest places of the province; and he shall do that which his fathers have not done, nor his fathers' fathers; he shall scatter among them the prey, and spoil, and riches: yea, and he shall forecast his devices against the strong holds, even for a time" (see Daniel 11:24).

He will be identified by Christians, though he is unrecognized as such by the rest of mankind.

"Let no man deceive you by any means: for that day shall not come, except there come a falling away first, and that man of sin be revealed, the son of perdition;" (II Thessalonians 2:3).

And, he will be called "The Assyrian."

"There thus saith the Lord God of hosts, O my people that dwellest in Zion, be not afraid of the Assyrian: he shall smite thee with a rod, and shall lift up his staff against thee, after the manner of Egypt" (Isaiah 10:24).

"And this man shall be the peace, when the Assyrian shall come into our land: and when he shall tread in our palaces, then shall we raise against him seven shepherds, and eight principal men" (Micah 5:5).

We are already seeing now how the desire for global peace is leading to the rise of a single governing force (currently the United Nations), and is headed to a place where a politician of inordinate appeal and power could control world opinion.

The recent NEW WORLD ORDER that mobilized to attack Iraq is indicative of the type of thinking the nation's leaders are now considering.

The leader who comes out of the New Roman empire will assert his world ambitions by taking on the most troubling problem - the Middle East crisis. The chaos of nations after the battle of Ezekiel 38-39 - often referred to as World War III - will suggest to a war-weary world the need for a single ruler.

Out of this chaos the Antichrist will come up strong with a small people and skyrocket to international prominence as the man with the answers.

"He will oppose and will exalt himself over everything that is called God or is worshipped, so that he sets himself up in God's temple, proclaiming himself to be God" (II Thessalonians 2:4, NIV).

For a period of 3 1/2 years, God will allow the Antichrist to have power and authority over the nations of the world. It will be a time of great affliction and persecution for those not accepting his identification mark.

Throughout the world, it will be a time of drought, pestilence and worldwide famine. No one will be able to buy or sell unless they have the mark on their right hand or forehead.

> *"And he causeth all, both small and great, rich and poor, free and bond, to receive a mark in their right hand, or in their foreheads:*
> *"And that no man might buy or sell, save he that had the mark, or the name of the beast, or the number of his name"* *(Revelation 13:16-17).*

Ultimately, the Antichrist is overcome.

> *"And they overcame him by the blood of the Lamb, and by the word of their testimony; and they loved not their lives unto the death" (Revelation 12:11).*

In review, the Antichrist will make a seven-year covenant with Israel, guaranteeing her national security. This security from Arab opposition will be necessary, and prepare the way for the rebuilding of the Jewish Temple.

Until the Antichrist arrives, and signs the treaty with Israel, the Jewish Temple will not be rebuilt.

CHAPTER TEN

REBUILDING THE TEMPLE

According to Ezekiel 40-48, which significantly follows the story of the destruction of the Russian-led confederation as it attempts to invade Israel, the new Temple is necessary for the Antichrist's later appearance there.

Approximately 100 steps behind the Wailing Wall is located the Dome of the Rock, or the Mosque of Omar. It is to Islam what St. Peter's in Rome is to the Roman Catholics.

Despite the current existence of the Dome of the Rock, according to Revelation 11:1-2, a Jewish temple will be in existence in Jerusalem in the closing days of the age.

It will be built by the time of the Great tribulation.

> *"And there was given me a reed like unto a road: and the angel stood, saying, Rise, and measure the temple of God, and the altar, and them that worship therein. But the court which is without the temple leave out, and measure it not; for it is given unto the Gentiles: and the holy city shall they tread under foot forty and two months."*

It will be constructed on its original site.

According to the Law of Moses, the only place the Jewish temple can be built is upon Mount Moriah, where the first two temples were erected.

One major obstacle right now is that the third holiest place of the Muslim faith, the Dome of the Rock, is squarely in the middle of the old Temple site, and has been there for thirteen centuries!

Obviously, its destruction would cause great concern for Muslims around the world.

But prophecy demands the Jewish Temple be rebuilt there!

Daniel speaks of the Prince who will make a covenant with the Jewish people and guarantee them religious freedom to make sacrifices and oblations.

> *"And he shall confirm the covenant with many for one week: and in the midst of the week he shall cause the sacrifice and the oblation to cease, and for the overspreading of abominations he shall make it desolate, even until the consummation, and that determined shall be poured upon the desolate" (Daniel 9:27).*

That can only be done in the Temple.

The prophet also predicted that after three-and-a-half years, the Temple would be desecrated by the Prince, the Antichrist, who would invade the inner sanctum and proclaim himself God.

SO IT IS A PROPHETIC AND BIBLICAL CERTAINTY THAT ULTIMATELY THE TEMPLE WILL BE REBUILT!

The Antichrist must reach an agreement with the Arab countries to make a valid covenant with Israel. There is no way a Jewish Temple can be rebuilt without some concession to Arab sensibilities.

Christians will recognize the Antichrist when he makes his covenant with Israel. At that time, Christians will know a time of great trouble lies ahead.

The Antichrist will reign in Jerusalem for three-and-a-half years after having broken a seven-year covenant with Israel halfway through.

> *"And he shall confirm the covenant with many for one week (seven years): and in the midst of the week (3 1/2 years) he shall cause the sacrifice and the oblation to cease, and for the overspreading of abominations he shall make it desolate, even until the consummation, and that determined shall be poured upon the desolate"* *(Daniel 9:27).*

He will devise and impose a solution which will be accepted. And peace will result, for three and a half years.

Then, the cataclysmic events which will climax at Armageddon will begin. The Bible says,

> *"When they shall say, Peace and safety; then sudden destruction cometh upon them, as travail upon a woman with child; and they shall not escape (I Thessalonians 5:3).*

In summary, the Antichrist will arise out of the new Roman Empire! His beast-kingdom of the last days will position him as a false world savior under the United States of Europe.

> *"I am come in my Father's name, and ye receive me not: if another shall come in his own name, him ye will receive"* *(John 5:43).*

AFTER the invasion of Israel by Russia (CIS), according to the prophecy in the book of Daniel, there will be a time lapse of about three and a half years, a time when the Jews rebuild the Temple.

The Antichrist will then refuse to allow further sacrifices or rituals at the Temple.

Instead, the Antichrist will commit the "abomination of desolation" by desecrating the holy of holies by using it as a platform to declare himself to be God, and demanding the worship of mankind.

CHAPTER ELEVEN

ISRAEL HOSTS
THE BATTLE OF ARMAGEDDON

After Russia's defeat by Israel, only two superpowers will remain: the combined forces of Western civilization, under the leadership of the Antichrist, will face the vast hordes of the Orient, probably under the Red Chinese war machine.

The previous Russian attack will probably give the Antichrist the excuse for full occupation of Israel under the guise of protection.

In the actual battle of Armageddon, fully one-third of the world population will die!

> "By these there was a third part of
> men killed, by the fire, and by the smoke,
> and by the brimstone (Revelation 9:15).

The BATTLE OF ARMAGEDDON will take place at Megiddo, near Nazareth (Revelation 16:16) - a great plain where countless battles have already been fought - over the plain of Jezreel, which extends from the Mediterranean to the Jordan.

Joel called it the "valley of Jehoshaphat."

War is inevitable.

It will take place at the time of Christ's return to earth with His saints.

> "And I saw heaven opened, and
> behold a white horse; and he that sat

upon him was called Faithful and True, and in righteousness he doth judge and make war. His eyes were as a flame of fire, and on his head were many crowns; and he had a name written, that no man knew, but he himself. And he was clothed with a vesture dipped in blood: and his name is called the Word of God. And the armies which were in heaven followed him upon white horses, clothed in fine linen, white and clean. And out of his mouth goeth a sharp sword, that with it he should smite the nations: and he shall rule them with a rod of iron: and he treadeth the winepress of the fierceness and wrath of Almighty God... And I saw the beast (Antichrist) and the kings of the earth, and their armies, gathered together to make war against him that sat on the horse, and against his army" (Revelation 19:11-15,19).

Terrible fighting will center around the city of Jerusalem.

"Behold, I will make Jerusalem a cup of trembling unto all the people round about, when they shall be in the siege both against Judah and against Jerusalem" (Zechariah 12:2).

Isaiah speaks of frightful carnage taking place south of Jerusalem (Isaiah 63:1-4).

John predicts so many people will be slaughtered in the conflict that blood will stand up to the horses' bridles for a total distance of 200 miles northward and southward of Jerusalem.

> *"And the winepress was trodden without the city, and blood came out of the winepress, even unto the horse bridles, by the space of a thousand and six hundred furlongs" (Revelation 14:20).*

Slaughter results in the Middle East.

Also, a world-wide shock wave will destroy the cities of the nations. In an instant, the great cities of the world will be gone.

> *"And the great city was divided into three parts, and the cities of the nations fell:" (Revelation 16:19).*

Ultimately, the armies of God defeat this confederacy of godless world government.

The remnant of nations that joined to battle against Christ will be slain by Christ's sword. The Antichrist and false prophet are cast into lake of fire, and Satan is bound for one thousand years.

> *"And then the lawless one (the Antichrist) will be revealed and the Lord Jesus will slay him with the breath of His mouth and bring him to an end by His appearing at His coming" (II Thessalonians 2:8, TLB).*

> *"These both were cast alive into a lake of fire burning with brimstone. And the remnant were slain with the sword of*

him that sat upon the horse, which sword proceeded out of his mouth: and all the fowls were filled with their flesh" (Revelation 19:20-21).

All war and rebellion cease for one thousand years.

"And I saw an angel come down from heaven, having the key of the bottomless pit and a great chain in his hand.

"And he laid hold on the dragon, that old serpent, which is the Devil, and Satan, and bound him a thousand years,

"And cast him into the bottomless pit, and shut him up, and set a seal upon him, that he should deceive the nations no more, till the thousand years should be fulfilled: and after that he must be loosed a little season" (Revelation 20:1-3).

In the prophecies of the downfall of Assyria, because of her oppression of Israel, there are many references to Assyria as being in the last days an enemy of Israel.

"That I will break the Assyrian in my land, and upon my mountains tread him under foot: then shall his yoke depart from off them, and his burden depart from off their shoulders" (Isaiah 14:25; Isaiah 10:20-27; 31:4-9; Micah 5:5,6).

The future Antichrist is called "the Assyrian," because he will rule the old Assyrian Empire territory when he comes (Isaiah 10:10-27; 30:18-33; 31:4-32:20; Micah 5:3-15).

The prophecies in these passages were recorded against the Assyrian king in the days of the prophets, but a study of them reveals that they have a latter-day fulfillment in the future Assyrian king who is to oppress Israel just preceding her final restoration. The Assyrian territory will be part of the Antichrist's kingdom and in that sense he is the king of Assyria.

Israel, at the second coming of Christ, will be regathered from Assyria.

> *"I will bring them again also out of the land of Egypt, and gather them out of Assyria; and I will bring them into the land of Gilead and Lebanon; and place shall not be found for them.*
>
> *"And he shall pass through the sea with affliction, and shall smite the waves in the sea, and all the deeps of the river shall dry up: and the pride of Assyria shall be brought down, and the sceptre of Egypt shall depart away" (Zechariah 10:10-11).*

(Isaiah 11:10-16; 27:12,13; Matthew 24:31).
Assyria is to be blessed in the Millennium with Israel.

> *"And in that day thou shalt say, O LORD, I will praise thee: though thou wast angry with me, thine anger is turned*

away, and thou comfortedst me" (Isaiah 12:1).

Thus, we see Assyria in the kingdom of the beast or as part of the eighth kingdom as to territory and peoples.

At the moment, there are large numbers of hopeless Assyrian refugees in camps in Greece, Germany, Spain, Cyprus, Turkey and other European countries waiting for their unknown destination. More than 80,000 Assyrian refugees have entered the U.S. to enjoy the safety and opportunities given to them in this country of freedom. A large number of these people are living with hope that now is the time that America will assist them in gaining their long-denied rights as equal citizens in Iraq, their ancestral homeland.

On August 5, 1991, the Assyrians were formally accepted as members of the Unrepresented Nations and Peoples Organization (UNPO) at the 2nd Assembly of this new organization which was founded in the Hague, The Netherlands in February, 1991.

From 612 BC to 1991 AD is a long time to wait!

It was a historic day for the Assyrians. Is this the first step in the prophecy restoring Assyria as recorded in Isaiah 19:23-25?

> "In that day there will be a highway from Egypt to Assyria. The Assyrians will go to Egypt and the Egyptians to Assyria. The Egyptians and Assyrians will worship together.

> "In that day Israel will be the third, along with Egypt and Assyria, a blessing on the earth.
> "The Lord Almighty will bless them, saying, 'Blessed be Egypt my people, Assyria my handiwork, and Israel my inheritance'" (Isaiah 19:23-25, NIV).

Throughout the world, many nations and peoples like the Assyrians struggle to regain their lost countries, maintain their cultural identity, and establish basic human and economic rights.

In the case of the Assyrians, they are second-class citizens in the land of their ancestors. The Assyrians have sacrificed greatly to gain the independence of their homeland, and despite their pure loyalty they offered to the Allied cause, and especially to protect the interest of Great Britain, the Assyrians lost hope of ever having the most basic human rights which they once enjoyed in their high and now inaccessible homeland in the Hakkari mountains.

The Baath Regime, under the atrocious leadership of Saddam Hussein, has shown new measures of aggression against the Assyrian people. Under his command the Iraqi forces have already bombarded and devastated numerous Assyrian villages in the North of Iraq. A great number of their historical churches and monasteries have been leveled to the ground.

The Assyrians have been deprived of the right to practice and preserve their culture and language. Their able-bodied men have been dragged into the army and put into the front lines to rage an unwitting fight against the Kurds, Iran and Kuwait.

Cruel and inhumane atrocities inflicted upon the innocent Assyrian people have forced these unfortunate hordes to flee and leave their homes and belongings and escape their homeland.

This process has been taking place for over two decades.

In summary, here is the brief biblical history of how God has used Assyria and Israel together in the past, and how He will use them in the future:

1. Assyria is first mentioned as oppressing Israel in the reign of Menahem when Israel was put under tribute (2 Kings 15:16-20).

2. Assyria invaded Israel in the reign of Pekah (2 Kings 15:27-31).

3. Assyria formed an alliance with Judah against Israel (2 Kings 16).

4. Assyria took the ten tribes of Israel captive in 749 B.C. (2 Kings 17).

5. Assyria invaded Judah after the fall of Israel (2 Kings 18,19).

6. Next came wars between Egypt and Assyria for supremacy. During this time, Judah again fell into the hands of Egypt (2 Kings 23). Assyria oppressed Israel and Judah, periodically, for about 175 years.

7. In the prophecies of the downfall of Assyria because of her oppression to Israel, there are many references to Assyria as being in the last days an enemy of Israel (Isaiah 10:20-27; 14:25; 31:4-9; Micah 5:5,6).

8. The future Antichrist is called "the Assyrian," because he will rule the old Assyrian Empire territory when he comes.

9. Israel at the second coming of Christ will be regathered from Assyria (Isaiah 11:10-16; 27:12,13; Zechariah 10:10,11; Matthew 24:31).

10. Assyria is blessed in the Millennium with Israel (Isaiah 11:16; 19:23-25),"God's Plan For Man."

Remember, Jesus said:

"The men of Nineveh shall rise in judgment with this generation, and shall condemn it:" (Matthew 12:41).

Ancient Assyria, along with Egypt, was the great early Middle Eastern empire. Its principal territory coincided with modern Iraq and Syria. To fulfill Isaiah's prophecy, Syria and Iraq must merge into one entity, possibly called Assyria, which will in turn make peace with Israel and then experience a profound spiritual revival.

A merger of Syria and Iraq was attempted at the beginning of 1979, but the initial undertaking was aborted. Undoubtedly, one of the key prophetic areas to watch will be in Syria and Iraq as "Assyria" begins to move toward God's plan.

Currently, the Assyrians are scattered, and no man can gather them - it will take the power of almighty God.

"Thy shepherds slumber, O king of Assyria; thy nobles shall dwell in the dust; thy people is scattered upon the mountains, and no man gathereth them" (Nahum 3:18).

As a miracle of miracles, Aramaic and most of the ancient Biblical customs which were common to

Assyrian people have survived in northern Iraq today. Aramaic is still spoken in Iraq and in northwestern Iran by remnants of the Assyrian people and the Jews of the exile.

The Assyrians have now been without a country for 2600 years, yet they have maintained their identity. There are only two ancient countries that have been without a country for thousands of years and yet maintain their identity.

The Israelites have regained their country.

God has a plan for the Israelites as he does for the Assyrians.

Believers who are realistic and see the Assyrians scattered all over the world with no political, financial or military power can only conclude it is through God's power that this prophecy can ever become a reality.

Today, Israel, greatly outnumbered and surrounded by the Arab world, exists by God's power and grace as a strong nation capable of maintaining its freedom as a people. The Israelis will turn to Christ the Messiah in the last days (Christ's second coming). At that time, Assyria will be a nation, and with Egypt, will befriend Israel.

Just as God blessed the Assyrians when they repented back in the days of Jonah, so also today it will happen once again!

I believe the day is soon coming when this prophetic word from Isaiah 60:22 (NIV) will soon be fulfilled:

> *"The least of you will become a thousand, the smallest a mighty nation. I am the LORD; in its time I will do this swiftly."*

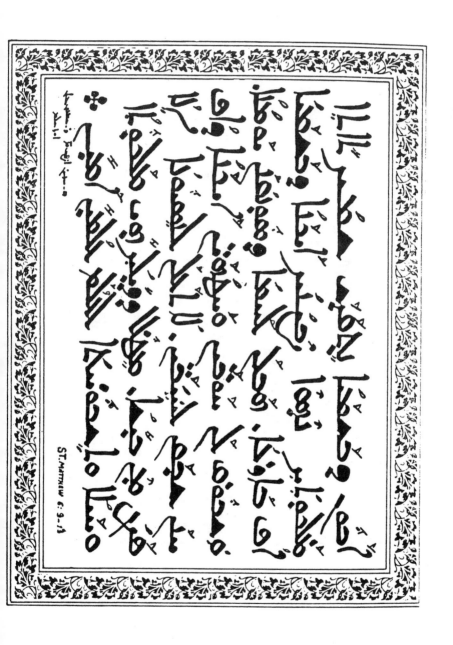

This is an Assyrian copy of the Lord's Prayer

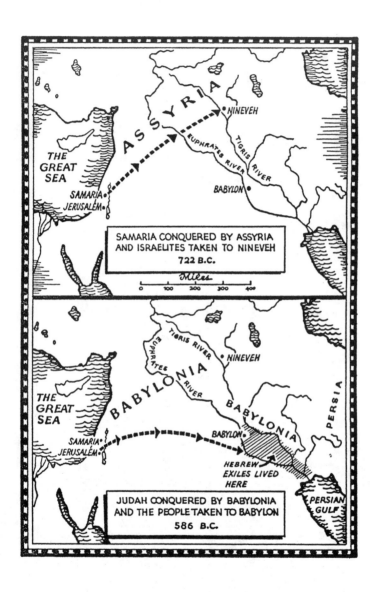

The dispersions of the Northern and Southern Kingdoms.

ASSYRIAN OR ARAMAIC WORDS
THAT APPEAR IN THE BIBLE

In Acts 21:40 and 22:2 (NIV), Paul the Apostle spoke to the Jews in Jerusalem in "Aramaic" (the King James versions says "Hebrew tongue"). Dake, in his Bible note, calls it "Chaldee-Syriac."

Daniel 5:25-28: Mene, Tekel, Parsin.

Mene: God has numbered the days of your reign and brought it to an end.

Tekel: You have been weighed on the scales and found wanting.

Peres: Your kingdom is divided and given to the Medes and Persians.

Matthew 5:22: Raca, which means "I spit on you." (Lamsa).

Matthew 6:24: Mammon, wealth, riches, money.

Matthew 27:46: "Eloi, Eloi, lama sabachthani?" which means, "My God, my God, why have you forsaken me?" (or, "For This I was kept," Lamsa).

Mark 5:41: "Talitha koum", which means "Little girl, I say to you, get up."

Mark 7:11: Corban, that is, "a gift devoted to God."

Mark 7:34: Ephphatha which means "be opened." (Eastern version: Ethpathakh) Lamsa.

John 19:13: "...The stone pavement" (which in Aramaic is Gabbatha). (NIV).

John 19:17: "The place of the skull" (NIV), in Aramaic is Golgotha.

John 19:20 (NIV), "...the sign was written in Aramaic, Latin and Greek."

John 20:16: Cried out in Aramaic, "Rabboni" (which means teacher).

Acts 1:19:   "They called that field in their language "akeldama" that is, "field of blood."

Acts 9:36: "In Joppa there was a disciple named Tabitha" (which, when translated, is Dorcas). NIV says both Tabitha (Aramaic) and Dorcas (Greek) mean "Gazelle."

Acts 21:40: "... he said to them in Aramaic... " (NIV).

Acts 22:2: "When they heard him speak to them in Aramaic..." (NIV).

Acts 26:14: I heard a voice saying to me in Aramaic, "Saul, Saul, why do you persecute me?" (NIV).

I Corinthians 16:22: Maranatha (KJV) "Our Lord, come".

Abba, Father, found in Mark 14:36; Romans 8:15; Galatians 4:6.

In Acts 6:1 (NIV), Luke mentions "the Aramaic speaking community."

Cephas, Aramaic for "rock," John 1:42;

I Corinthians 1:12; 3:22; 9:5; 15:5; Galatians 2:9.

Finally, the text in Daniel 2:4 through Chapter 7 is in Aramaic, as well as Ezra 4:8-6:18, and Jeremiah 10:11.   (The Old Testament Apocryphal Book of Judith is all about the Assyrian invasion of Jerusalem.)

ESTIMATED ASSYRIANS IN THE WORLD - 1992

Iraq	1,550,000
Syria	900,000
U.S.A.	290,000
Lebanon	245,000
Russia (now called C.I.S.)	135,000
Iran	73,000
Turkey	61,500
Sweden	24,000
Australia	24,500
Germany	21,500
United Kingdom	12,500
Holland	12,500
Canada	11,500
South America	8,500
France	7,500
Kuwait	6,900
Belgium	5,800
Switzerland	3,600
Greece	3,500
Italy	2,900
All other countries	375,000

Total World	3,773,200*

Assyrians include Chaldeans, Jacobites, Church of the East, and others.
* These numbers are estimates only from the National Assyrian American Business and Professional Directory, Chicago, Illinois, 1992.

Assyrians in the United States - 1992

Little Rock, Arkansas	4,000
Los Angeles, California	23,000
Modesto, California	10,000
Turlock, California	9,500
San Diego, California	4,500
San Francisco, California	8,000
Other California	11,500
Chicago, Illinois	68,000
North Eastern Indiana	8,000
Boston, Mass./Hartford, Conn. Area	9,500
Detroit, Michigan	45,500
Flint, Michigan	4,000
Other Michigan	11,000
Elizabeth, New Jersey	6,000
New York, New York	9,500
Yonkers, New York	11,500
Philadelphia, Pennsylvania	6,500
Other U.S.A.	40,000

TOTAL U.S.A.   296,000 *

* These numbers are estimates only, and also include Chaldeans, Jacobites, Church of the East and others.

The Assyrian Empire From 824 TO 625 B.C.

ASSYRIAN ALPHABET

Not joined to preceding letter.	Joined to preceding letter.	Estrangéla.	Name of letter.
ܐ (ܐ final)	ܐ ܐ (ܐ final)	ܐ	ܐܠܦ Alap
ܒ	ܒ	ܒ	ܒܝܬ Béith
ܓ	ܓ	ܓ	ܓܡܠ Gamal
ܕ	ܕ	ܕ	ܕܠܬ Dalath
ܗ	ܗ	ܗ	ܗܐ Hé or Hi
ܘ	ܘ	ܘ	ܘܘ Wau
ܙ	ܙ	ܙ	ܙܝܢ Zain
ܚ	ܚ	ܚ	ܚܝܬ Khéith
ܛ, ܛ	ܛ, ܛ	ܛ	ܛܝܬ Téith
ܝ	ܝ	ܝ	ܝܘܕ Yudb
ܟ (ܟ final)	ܟ (ܟ final)	ܟ	ܟܦ Kap
ܠ	ܠ	ܠ	ܠܡܕ Lamadh
ܡ (ܡ final)	ܡ (ܡ final)	ܡ	ܡܝܡ Mim
ܢ (ܢ final)	ܢ (ܢ final)	ܢ	ܢܘܢ Nun
ܣ	ܣ	ܣ	ܣܡܟܬ Simkath
ܥ	ܥ	ܥ	ܥܐ 'E
ܦ	ܦ	ܦ	ܦܐ Pé or Pi
ܨ	ܨ	ܨ	ܨܕܐ Şadbé
ܩ	ܩ	ܩ	ܩܘܦ Qop
ܪ	ܪ	ܪ	ܪܝܫ Resh
ܫ	ܫ	ܫ	ܫܝܢ Shin
ܬ, ܬ	ܬ, ܬ	ܬ	ܬܘ Tau

The Assyrian Alphabet

PROPHETS OF THE ASSYRIAN PERIOD

Jonah: Sent to warn the inhabitants of Nineveh (capital of Assyria) of God's judgement. As a result, the people changed their ways and God spared the city.

Amos: Born in Judah but prophesied in Israel during reign of Jeroboam II. Condemned Israel's neighboring countries for their cruelty, but mostly Israel for breaking God's laws. Warned that the Israelites would be taken captive by the Assyrians.

Hosea: In the years leading up to the fall of Samaria. Hosea warned that the people would become slaves in Assyria because they had forgotten God. They had even turned to Assyria and Egypt for help.

Isaiah: Lived in Jerusalem at the time when Judah was threatened by the Assyrians. Looked ahead not only to the deliverance of Jerusalem from the Assyrians but also to its conquest by the Babylonians and to a future age of peace.

Micah: Warned of the Assyrian and Babylonian invasions; predicted the fall of both Samaria and Jerusalem.

Zephaniah: Lived during Josiah's reign. Condemned the worship of Canaanite and Assyrian gods. Predicted disaster for the pagan nations around. Foretold the destruction and restoration of Jerusalem.

Nahum: Predicted the destruction of Nineveh as a judgement on the Assyrians for their cruel treatment of other nations.

SYRIAC VOCABULARY AS SPOKEN TODAY IN THE ASSYRIAN HOMES

Believe (to): limhaimoone
I believe: mhaimoone win
I will believe: bit mhaiminin
I believed: mhoominee
Confession: maodeta
Conversation: sohbat
Cross: sleeva
Die (to): limyata
Faith: haimanootha
False: ginaha
Fast (religious): soma
Fear: zdoota
Free: azad
Give (to): leeyava
I will give: bit yavin
I gave: yevilee
Given: peesha yoova
Government: hookma
Grandfather: savoona
Grandchildren: navigi
Help (to): limhayoore
I will help: bit mhayerin
I helped: mhooyeree
Honor: eegara
Hope: hevee
Important: lazim
Kind: mrakhamana
King: malka
Lady: khanim
Lamb: pera
Leader: mtagbirana

Learn (to): lilyapa
I will learn: bit yalpen
I learned: leeplee
To live: likhaya
I will live: bit khayin
I lived: khelee
Look (to): limgashooge
I will look: bit mgnshgin
I looked: mgooshiklee
Lord: mara
Love: khooba
Minister: wazeer
Mission: skleekhoota
Mistake: khilta
News: khabra khata
Obedience: masyatta
Obey (to) lmasyoote
I will obey: bit masyittin
I obeyed: moosyitlee
Parents: avake
Patience: khamalta
Peace: shlama
People: nashe
Poor: miskena
Possible: momkin
Praise (noun): khigra
Praise (to): likhgara
I will praise: bit khagrin
I praised: khgiree
Pray (to): limsalooye
I will pray: bit msalin
I prayed: msoolelee
Prayer: slootha
Present (gift): pashkash
Price: teema

Prophet: nveeya
Promise (noun): qowla
Promise (to make): limgawoole
Proof: sahdootha
Protect (to): lintara
Proud: mare shoovhara
Punishment: mtalamta
Question: mbagarta
Raise (to): lmaroome
Receive (to): limgaboole
Religion: mazhab
Remember (to): lidkhara
Return (to): lidyara
Reward: haqa
Right hand: yam meena
River: nahra
Road: oorkha
Room: otagh
Remember (to): lidkhara
Return (to): lidyara
Rich: dowlatmand
Say (to): lemara
See (to): likhzaya
Send (to): limshadoore
I will send: bit mshadrin
Sheep: erbe
Sick: mirya
Sing (to): lizmara
Sin: khteeta
Star: kaokhva
Talk (to): limhamzoome
Teach (to): lmaloope
I will teach: bit malpin
I taught: mooliplee
Teacher: malpana

Tell (to): limtangooye
I will tell: bit mtanin
I told: mtoonelee
Thank (to): litana minta
Think (to): likhshava
Touch (to): lidgara
Valuable: mare teema
Village: mata
Voice: khala
Wait (to): lispara
Walk (to): likhdara
Want (to): libaya
Way: oorkha
Weep (to): libkhaya
Widow: armilta
Wife: bakhta
Wind: pokha
Wine: khamra
Winter: sitwa
Wise: honana
Witness: sahdootha
Wolf: deva
Word: khabra
Work: poolkhana
World: doonye
Write (to): liktava
Writing: kthawta
Wrong: khilta
Yesterday: timmal or yoma d'vire.
Young: zoora or juanqa
God: Alaha
Jesus Christ: Eshoo M'shekha
Holy Spirit: Rokha Gutsha
Our Father in heaven: Baban bi shmeya
God bless you: Alaha barikhlookhun

ASSYRIA IN THE BIBLE

Origin of : Genesis 10:8-12,22.

Situated beyond the River Euphrates, Isa. 7:20.

Watered by the River Tigris, Gen. 2:14.

Called: The land of Nimrod, Micah 5:6. Shinar, Gen. 11:2. Asshur, Hosea 14:3.

Nineveh, chief city, Gen. 10:11; Jonah 1:1.

Symbolized by a lion, Jer.50:17,18; Nah. 2:11-13.

Conquered Egypt, Exodus 1:8; Isaiah 52:4.

Celebrated for: Fertility, II Kings 18:32; Extent of conquests, II Kings 18:33-35; 19:11-13; Isa. 10:9-14. Extensive commerce: Ezekiel 27:23,24.

As a power was: Formidable, Isa. 28:2. Cruel, Nah. 3:19. Destructive, Isa. 10:7. Proud and haughty, II Kings 19:22-24; Isa. 10:8.

An instrument of God's vengeance, Isa. 7:20; 10:5,6.

Chief men of, described: Ezek. 23:6,12,23.

Armies of, described: Isa. 5:26-29.

King Tiglath-Pileser (Pul): Invaded Israel, II Kings 15:19. Bought off by Menahem, II Kings 15:19,20. Ravaged Israel, II Kings15:29. Asked to aid Ahaz against Syria, II Kings 16:7,8. Conquered Syria, II Kings 16:9.

King Shalmaneser: Reduced Israel to tribute, II Kings 17:3. Imprisoned Hoshea, II Kings 17:4. Carried Israel captive, II Kings 17:5,6. Re-peopled Samaria from Assyria, II Kings 17:24.

King Tiglah-Pileser (Pul): II Kings 15:199-20,29; 16:7-9.

King Shalmaneser: II Kings 17:3-6, 24.

King Sennacherib: II Kings 18:13-19:37

The re-peopling of Samaria from Assyria completed by King Ashurbanipal, Ezra 4:10.

Jerusalem and Smaria rebuked for following the idolatries of: Ezekiel 16:28; 23.

The greatness, extent, duration, and fall of, illustrated, Ezek. 31:3-17.

Predictions concerning Assyria: Conquest of the Kenites, Num. 24:22. Of Syria, Isa. 8:4. Of Israel, Isa. 8:4; Hosea 9:3; 10:6; 11:5. Invasion of Judah, Isa. 5:26; 7:17-20; 8:8; 10:5,6,12. Restoration of Israel, Isa. 27:12,13; Hos. 11:11; Zech. 10:10.

Destruction of: Isa. 10:12-19; 14:24,25; 30:31-33; 31:8,9; Zech. 10:11.

Participation in the blessings of the Lord: Isa. 19:23-25; (The work of God's hands").

BIBLIOGRAPHY

Books

ASSYRIAN CHURCH CUSTOMS, Surma D'Bait Mar Shimun, Edited by W.A. Wigram, D.D., 1920

ASSYRIAN SCULPTURE, Julian Reade, British Museum Publications Ltd., London, England, 1983

ASSYRIAN SELF-TEACHER, Volume One, William Sarmas, Cannes, France

BY FOOT TO CHINA, Dr. John M.L. Young, Tokyo Radio Press, 1984 (History of the Church of the East)

COLLOQUIAL SYRIAC, Lieut. R. Hart, M.B.E., Mosul Assyrian Press, Chicago, IL, 1926

DAKE'S ANNOTATED REFERENCE BIBLE, Finis Jennings Dake, Dake Bible Sales, Inc., Atlanta, GA, 1963

DOCUMENTS FROM OLD TESTAMENT TIMES, Edited by D. Winton Thomas, Harper and Row, New York, 1961

FROM IRAQ TO ARMAGEDDON, Keith Intrater, Destiny Image Publishers, Shippensburg, PA, 1991

GODS' PLAN FOR MAN, Rev. Finis Jennings' Dake, Dake Bible Sales, Inc., Lawrenceville, GA 1949

HISTORY OF THE SYRIAN NATION AND THE OLD EVANGELICAL - APOSTOLIC CHURCH OF THE EAST, Prof. George David Malech, Minneapolis, MN

HOLY BIBLE FROM THE PESHITTA - THE AUTHORIZED BIBLE OF THE CHURCH OF THE EAST, George M. Lamsa, A.J. Holman Co., Nashville, TN, 1957

INTERNATIONAL BIBLE DICTIONARY, Logos International, Plainfield, NJ, 1977

JOSEPHUS - THE JEWISH WAR, G.A. Williamson, translator, Penguin Books, Baltimore, MD, 1974

LAND OF THE LION AND THE SUN, Absalom D. Shabaz, Published by the author, Milwaukee, WI, 1901 and 1904

MINORITIES IN THE ARAB WORLD, A.H. Hourani, Oxford University Press, London, New York, Toronto, 1947

MY NEIGHBOR JESUS, George M. Lamsa, Aramaic Bible Center, Inc., San Antonio, TX 78246, 1932

NATIONAL ASSYRIAN AMERICAN BUSINESS AND PROFESSIONAL DIRECTORY, CHICAGO, IL, 1990 and 1992

NAVE'S TOPICAL BIBLE, Orville J. Nave, Moody Press, Chicago, IL 1921

OLD TESTAMENT SURVEY, William Lasor, David Hubbard, Frederic Bush, William B. Eerdmans Publishing Co., Grand Rapids, MI 1982

OPERATION BABYLON, Shlomo Hillel, Doubleday

ORAHAM'S DICTIONARY OF THE ASSYRIAN LANGUAGE AND ENGLISH, Alexander Joseph Oraham, Mic. D. Consolidated Press (Assyrian Press of America), Chicago, IL 1943

OUR YESTERDAY, TODAY, AND TOMORROW, Peter H. Talia, 1980

POCKET BIBLE HANDBOOK, Henry H. Halley, Eighteenth Edition Revised, Henry H. Halley, Chicago, IL, 1948

READER'S DIGEST ATLAS OF THE BIBLE, The Readers Digest Assoc., Inc. Pleasantville, NY, 1981

REPUBLIC OF FEAR, Samer al-Khalil, Pantheon Books, NY, 1990

TEACH YOURSELF ARAMAIC, Dr. Mar Aprem, Mar Narsai Press, Trichur, Kerala, India, 1981

THE ASSYRIANS AND THEIR NEIGHBOURS, Rev. W.A. Wigram, G. Bell and Sons, London, 1929

THE ASSYRIAN TRAGEDY, Mar Eshai Shimun XXIII, Annemasse, 1934

THE BLOOD OF THE MOON - THE ROOTS OF THE MIDDLE EAST CRISIS, George Grant, Wolgemuth and Hyatt, Brentwood, TN, 1991

THE BRITISH BETRAYAL OF THE ASSYRIANS, Yusuf Malek, The Assyrian National Foundation, Chicago, IL

THE DEATH OF A NATION, Abraham Yohannan, Ph.D., G.P. Putnam's Sons, NY and London, 1916

THE HOLY BIBLE, New International Version, Zondervan Bible Publishers, Grand Rapids, MI, 1979

THE INTERNATIONAL STANDARD BIBLE ENCYCLOPEDIA, James Orr, General Editor, Vol. I, Wm. B. Eerdmans Publishing Co. Grand Rapids, MI 1974

THE LION ENCYCLOPEDIA OF THE BIBLE, Lion Publishing Corp., Batavia, IL, 1986

THE LIVING BIBLE, Tyndale House Publishers, Wheaton, IL 1971

THE NESTORIANS OR THE LOST TRIBES, Asahel Grant, 1840

THE NEW COMPACT BIBLE DICTIONARY, T. Alton Bryant, Editor, Zondervan Publishing House, Grand Rapids, MI 1967

THE OLD TESTAMENT SPEAKS, Samuel J. Schultz, Harper & Row, NY 1960

THE OLDEST CHRISTIAN PEOPLE, William Emhardt and George Lamsa, AMS Press, NY, 1926

THE RAGE OF ISLAM, Yonan H. Shahbaz, The Judson Press, Philadelphia

Periodicals

ARAMCO WORLD MAGAZINE, Aramco, Washington, D.C.

ASSYRIAN GUARDIAN, Assyrian Guardian, Inc., Chicago, IL

ASSYRIAN UNIVERSAL ALLIANCE FOUNDATION NEWSLETTER, Assyrian Universal Foundation, Chicago, IL

MATHIBANA, Bulletin of Information, France, 1974

THE ASSYRIAN STAR, The Assyrian Star Inc., Chicago, IL

VOICE OF ASSYRIANS, Chicago, IL

Papers

"A Comparative Study of the Form and Function of Assyrian and Egyptian Architecture," Sharon Wells Booko, Independent Study in Humanities paper, Barat College of The Sacred Heart, Lake Forest, Illinois, April 1985

"A Rock in Iraq," Rev. Kenny Joseph, Tokyo, Japan

League of Nations, Official Journal, Special Supplement No. 143, Geneva, 1935

"Assyrian Nation in the Great War," Part One and Two.

"The Assyrian Nation After the Great War," Part One (1920-1932), Part Two (Jan. - July, 1935) compiled by Dr. Emanuel Yousip Kamber,
Kalamazoo, MI

"A Brief History of the Assyrian Nation," G.M. Dooman, 1942

Assyrians: A Synopsis, Assyrian Universal Alliance Foundation, Chicago, IL

Assyrians, The Ashurbanipal Library, Chicago, IL

"Church of the East," Esho S. Marcus, D.M.D., B.D.S.

"Assyria and Assyrian in the Bible," Rev. John Booko, Three Rivers, MI

"The Assyrian Bonfire of February," Gewargis M. Yaco

"Our Smallest Ally," Rev. W.A. Wegram

"The Tragedy of the Assyrians," Lt. Col. R.S. Stafford

"Who Are Assyrians" William Daniel

"God's Plan for the Assyrians" John Yonan

"Kha-B'Nissan, Assyrian New Year," Dr. Emanuel Yousip Kamber, Kalamazoo, MI

"Assyria's End," William H. Shea, Ph.D., Berrien Springs, MI, 1980

Articles

"The Assyrian Nationhood," David B. Perley, The Assyrian Star, Jan./Feb. 1971

"There will be an Assyria," Assyrian Sentinel, Vol. 3, No. 3, June 1978, Hartford, Conn.

"Ashor, Khoshaba Pnuel," The Assyrian Star

"Immortal Beasts," Time, May 9, 1960

"Custodian For the Fertile Crescent, " Time, March 31, 1967

"The Assyrians of Iran" Reunification of a Millat," 1906-1914, Eden Naby, The Assyrian Star."

"Are the Assyrians a Nation?", Mark Thomas, The Assyrian Star, Nov.-Dec., 1971

"Away From Iraq, Assyrians Try to Retain Identity," Andrew Cassel, The Philadelphia Inquirer, Feb. 16, 1991

"Exile on State Street," Paul Glastris, U.S. News and World Report, p. 15, Feb. 11, 1991

"Hope For a Homeland," Stephen Franklin, Chicago Tribune, Jan. 10, 1991

"Urgent Assistance Required For Assyrian Refugees in Cyprus," R.J. Rushdoony, Chalcedon Report, No. 316, Nov. 1991, Vallecto, CA

"The History of Our Language," William Sarmas, The Assyrian Star

"Aramaic, Syriac or Assyrian," Haido Yuarish, The Assyrian

"A Brief Study in the Aramaic Language, Isaac Ibrahim," The Assyrian Star, May-June 1974, p. 21

"The Language of Jesus is a Living Tongue: Aramaic Spoken Still by Church of the East." The Protestant Voice, Nov. 14, 1947

"Assyrian Church of the East." Victor Wales, The Assyrian

"Light From the East," Irwen St. John Tucker, The Protestant Voice, Dec. 26, 1947

"Christmas and Christianity An Assyrian Heritage," S.M.

"The Assyrian Church Under the Sasanian and Muslim Rulers," Emanuel Kamber, The Assyrian

"Tatian the Assyrian," John Booko, Northern Baptist Theological Seminary, Chicago, IL 1948

"Nestorius," John Booko, Northern Baptist Theological Seminary, Chicago, IL 1949

Video Tapes

Phases of Civilization An Assyrian Legacy, Prototype Productions, Assyrian - American Federation, Inc.

Assyrian Destiny in the Middle East, John Yonan, Chicago, IL, 1980

Assyria - The Forgotten Nation In Prophecy, Reverend John Booko, 200 S. Hooker Avenue, Three Rivers, MI 49093, 1992.

Audio

Assyria in Prophecy, Rev. John Booko, Intercessors For America Lifeline, Seattle, WA, 1991

Assyria and Iraq, Rev. John Booko, Three Rivers Christian Fellowship, P.O. Box 422, Three Rivers, Michigan 49093, 1991

The Language of Jesus, Rev. John Booko, Three Rivers Christian Fellowship, 1992

Other Tapes by John Booko

Assyria and God's Grace
The Assyria/Israel Connection
Assyrian Vocabularies
Assyria and its Language in the Bible

103D CONGRESS
1ST SESSION

H. J. RES. ___

IN THE HOUSE OF REPRESENTATIVES

Mr. GUTIERREZ introduced the following joint resolution; which was referred to the Committee on _____

JOINT RESOLUTION

Expressing the sense of Congress to establish "Assyrian Pride and Remembrance Day" to recognize the tremendous legacy of the Assyrian community and to encourage all Americans to participate in the commemoration.

Whereas the Assyrian people have a proud history around the world and in the United States, dating to the earliest moments of civilization;

Whereas the Assyrian people desire, above all else, to live in peace with their neighbors;

Whereas Americans of Assyrian heritage have contributed demonstrably to the well-being of all in the United States through hard work, sympathy for others, and maintenance of unique cultural traditions;

140

Whereas the history of Assyrians consists of triumphant memories as well as painful ones, including the tragic massacre at Simel;

Whereas the Assyrian people have persevered in spite of such sadness, and have, indeed, thrived in a full range of endeavors undertaken as a whole and as individuals;

Whereas Assyrians have long been allies of the United States, adding vitally to victory in the First World War and to the continued struggle for peace;

Whereas the United States is a Nation that welcomes, and depends upon, people of all backgrounds, each with a story to offer others, from which America is able to craft itself into a Nation that is the envy of the world; and

Whereas all Americans, young and old, would benefit from a stronger knowledge of the Assyrian experience: Now, therefore, be it

1   *Resolved by the Senate and House of Representatives*
2   *of the United States of America in Congress assembled,*
3   That August 7, 1993, be recognized nationwide as "Assyr-
4   ian Pride and Remembrance Day," an occasion for all
5   Americans to appreciate the contributions, culture, and
6   history of the Assyrian community. The President is au-
7   thorized and requested to issue a proclamation calling
8   upon the people of the United States to observe the day
9   with appropriate ceremonies and activities.

A Final Note
Aiding Present Day Assyrians

There are thousands of Assyrians who had to leave their homes along with the Kurds in the aftermath of the unfortunate Gulf War. Even though most have returned, many found their homes destroyed. Years after the war, there are still many Assyrians who live in tents and shanty houses. They don't want to leave their ancestral homeland and form another wave of refugees begging for visas at the door steps of foreign embassies. They would rather endure hardship and rebuild their lives on the ashes of what once was called their home. But, without our spiritual and financial support, how long can they endure?

Should you, or your church, club or foundation, desire to help our Assyrian Christian brethren in Northern Iraq who are suffering from the attacks of the Iraqi Moslem regime and the prejudice of the Kurds and are lacking many of the bare essentials of life for their children - especially food, milk, and clothing, please send your financial donations to the "Assyrian Relief Fund" in care of my address, and I will see that it goes to the right destination.

"ALAHA BARIKH-LOOKH-UN RAHBA" (God bless you much).

ABOUT THE AUTHOR

John Booko, Sr. is an American born Assyrian whose parents were born in Northern Iraq; he speaks the Assyrian language. Reverend Booko holds a Bachelor of Theology degree from Northern Baptist Seminary in Oakbrook, Illinois, and a Master of Arts degree from Northwestern University Graduate School in Evanston, Illinois.

He is an ordained Baptist minister having served in Baptist Churches for 24 years. In 1975 he founded the Three Rivers Christian Fellowship, an interdenominational Church, where he serves the Lord with his son, Paul. He and his wife, Burnell, have resided in Three Rivers, Michigan since 1963. They have four children and fourteen grandchildren.

John also serves as the Regional Representative for "Intercessors for America," a ministry encouraging effective prayer and fasting for the church, our nation, and their leaders. His Trans/Local ministry is to build unity among pastors and to bless and encourage other churches and ministries.

In May of 1983, he travelled to Israel at the invitation of the government's Herut Party and met with Prime Minister, Menachem Begin in his office in Jerusalem.

In April of 1985, he was invited to Egypt by the Egyptian Foundation. In Cairo, Egypt, he visited with Egyptian President Hosni Mubarak in his Presidential Palace, and prayed with him.

THE WORLD MUST KNOW THAT ASSYRIA IS THE MISSING LINK IN GOD'S TRIANGLE FOR PEACE IN THE MIDDLE EAST! (ASSYRIA, ISRAEL, AND EGYPT)

> In that day there will be a highway from Egypt to Assyria, and the Assyrian will come into Egypt, and the Egyptian into Assyria, and the Egyptians will worship with the Assyrians. In that day Israel will be the third with Egypt and Assyria, a blessing in the midst of the earth, whom the Lord of hosts has blessed, saying, 'Blessed be Egypt my people, and Assyria the work of my hands, and Israel my heritage.'
>
> —ISAIAH 19:23-25 (RSV)

SHOULD YOU DESIRE TO HAVE ME SPEAK ON THE SUBJECT OF MY BOOK AT YOUR CHURCH, SCHOOL, CLUB OR ORGANIZATION, PLEASE FEEL FREE TO CONTACT ME AT THE ADDRESS LISTED ON THE BACK COVER OF THIS BOOK.